Praise for
Mudgirls Manifesto

We have hit a wall. In the Anthropocene, humanity's collective impact on
the biosphere undermines the very things that keep us alive — clean air,
water, soil, and biodiversity. We need a revolution away from the
corporate-political prioritization of the economy. *Mudgirls Manifesto* is a
glimpse of the way we all have to go — build community with shared
values and purpose, learn new skills and have fun doing it, don't be cowed
by experts, accept that hard work and healthy bodies go hand-in-hand,
and be confident knowing this is what must be done.
— David Suzuki

It is easy to forget, especially at the end of the day after trowelling
smooth another lumpy wall or sifting yet another wheelbarrow of clay, the
larger story behind the screen that keeps one caring, hopeful, and inspired.
The Mudgirls Manifesto reminded me of that story — my story, our story;
as women, mothers, and sisters we have the power to come together to
build a world in which we full-heartedly belong as equals, sculpting every
inch of our lives with all the beauty and integrity we so crave —
one bale, one bucket of mud at a time.
— Athena Steen, co-author, *The Straw Bale House*

As a natural builder, I couldn't agree more to the tenets laid out in this
book. Community, claiming the right to create our own shelter, the freedom
to make our own choices — bring out the "new normal" — all this is very
much at the core of the natural building movement. Let's not lose sight of
this as natural building materials and techniques inch their way into com-
mercial construction. This book speaks from my heart and clearly re-inspires
my work ethics. But there's more: an organizational structure that is at the
core inclusive and non-hierarchical and it works! Wonderfully woven and
written in an engaged, lively voice, it awakens my passion for working with
women's wisdom. Let it sink in — there are many levels of activism at work
here. And once you get it ... join this revolution. It's better for all of us.
— Elke Cole, Mudwoman and natural building consultant

This is a wonderful and inspiring and heartfelt book by a bunch of women who have taken a good measure of their lives into their own hands. These women are broadcasting their independent philosophy from British Columbia, but it's going to inspire girls and women all over the world. Why not build it myself? Why not use natural materials? Why not now?

— Lloyd Kahn, author,
Shelter and Builders of the Pacific Coast

For women wishing they could own a deliciously designed, custom-made dwelling they can actually afford, this is the book for you. For groups wanting to empower themselves with methods that bring joy (and success) to community organizing: ditto. For those of us trying to figure out how to reverse the direction of a society that's become increasingly greedy, techno-restrictive, and oppressive — guess what? It's all here. Incredibly engagingly written, with every contingency addressed — from what to do about the group power-freak to how to make starch paste. Talk about multi-tasking — there has never been a book quite like this. I'm enormously cheered up, and you will be too.

— Holly Dressel, co-author with David Suzuki, *Good News for a Change*,
More Good News, and *From Naked Ape to Superspecies*

It is so heartening to read the Mudgirls' story in these times of environmental collapse, increasing poverty, and overwhelming confusion. The Mudgirls are making homes that are gentle on the environment, enriching the lives of inhabitants and builders while encouraging community spirit. On top of all that, they are — lucky for us — sharing the experience with us in this upliftingly honest tale. Thank you!!

— Becky Bee, author, *The Cob Builders Handbook*

I am an admirer of the Mudgirls, for their incredible, creative natural building work, and even more their revolutionary village-building and social justice vision. They are full-spectrum builders of what matters most. In fact, I wish that I, too, could be a Mudgirl. For those of you who feel as I do, there is now a book that will help us join the cause. I hope your hands are muddy as you hold this copy of the *Mudgirls Manifesto!!*

— Mark Lakeman, co-founder,
City Repair and the Village Building Convergence

Stories inspire us to start our days, to live bigger lives, to build houses, to raise healthy children. Stories are important for our development. *Mudgirls Manifesto* is full of stories, stories that inspire new ways to live. The stories of free childcare at jobsites were revolutionary and inspiring for me. Not only do the Mudgirls inspire with their stories, they share their technological experience with natural building materials, tools, and client relations.
Thank you.

— Sukita Reay Crimmel, a Mudgirl in Portland, Oregon,
and author, *Earthen Floors*

Wow, if only this book was around when I was getting started! As a woman and as a long-time natural builder, this book is invaluable for any woman interested in the craft of Earth-centered building! It is a wonderful testament to what could be, what should be, and hells bells, what will be! They have woven the gritty truth of being a woman builder with how to do it in a supportive and nurturing, exemplary way, all with a much-needed declaration to smashing capitalism! My hope is that this book sparks a revolution of Mudgirls everywhere!

— Lydia Doleman, author,
Essential Light Straw Clay Construction

MUDGIRLS MANIFESTO

HANDBUILT HOMES • HANDCRAFTED LIVES

the mudgirls natural building collective

new society
PUBLISHERS

Printed in Canada. First printing April 2018

Inquiries regarding requests to reprint all or part of *Mudgirls Manifesto* should be addressed to New Society Publishers at the address below. To order directly from the publishers, please call toll-free (North America) 1-800-567-6772, or order online at www.newsociety.com

Any other inquiries can be directed by mail to:
New Society Publishers
P.O. Box 189, Gabriola Island, BC V0R 1X0, Canada
(250) 247-9737

LIBRARY AND ARCHIVES CANADA CATALOGUING IN PUBLICATION

Mudgirls Natural Building Collective, author
      Mudgirls manifesto : handbuilt homes, handcrafted lives
/ the Mudgirls Natural Building Collective.

Includes bibliographical references and index.
Issued in print and electronic formats.
ISBN 978-0-86571-877-7 (softcover).--ISBN 978-1-55092-670-5 (PDF).--ISBN 978-1-77142-265-9 (EPUB)

    1. Ecological houses. 2. Earth houses. 3. Sustainable buildings.

    4. Sustainable living. 5. Mudgirls Natural Building Collective. I. Title.

TH4860.M83 2018   728'.047   C2018-901248-X
                                    C2018-901249-8

Funded by the Government of Canada   Financé par le gouvernement du Canada

New Society Publishers' mission is to publish books that contribute in fundamental ways to building an ecologically sustainable and just society, and to do so with the least possible impact on the environment, in a manner that models this vision.

FSC MIX
Paper from responsible sources
FSC® C016245
www.fsc.org

Certified B Corporation

new society PUBLISHERS

Contents

PART I: A HISTORY WRITTEN IN MUD

> *Guiding Principle: We mostly work with unprocessed natural and recycled materials to create and decorate beautiful and healthy structures that are earth friendly.*
>
> *Guiding Principle: We believe this work is so important that we cannot wait until we are all experts. No matter the level of experience, we value each individual for their contribution and abilities and believe strongly in skill-building on the worksite.*

Acknowledgments

*T*HANKS FOR SAWING ...
Unending gratitude goes to every one of these people. If it had not been for the commitment, encouragement, passion, bravery, sweat, tears, the brilliance, the laughter, and love that these individual members gave to the formation and continuation of this collective, this book and this journey we are still on would be not be what it is today.

In no particular order, these people were part of what has made the Mudgirls a real-life, beautiful, ever-changing thing. Thank you for all you have done and all you still do.

> Jen Gobby, Auguste Mann, Emily Watson, Julie Chadwick, Sarah Segal, Karin Beviere, Jill Foreman, Amber Hieb, Su Donovaro, Gwen Gorrie, Bec McGuire, Bethany Scott, Jen Poole, Paula Johnson, Sheera Cipilinski, Nydia Solis, Anna Himmelman, Mireille Evans, Ginette Massey, Robyn Ave, Chrys LoSerbo

These fine people are currently keeping the Mudgirls up and running with kindness and diligence; they also wrote this book.

> Clare Kenny, Molly Murphy, Amanda-Rae Hergesheimer, Rose Dickson, Chelsey Braham, Melisande Chagnon, Amber Hamilton, Nina Bell, Yolanda Laking, Rosie Graham, Sophie Randell

Introduction

Another world is not only possible, she is on her way. On a quiet day, I can hear her breathing.

— Arundhati Roy

By Jen Gobby

*F*OR OVER A DECADE NOW, The Mudgirls Collective has been building healthy, eco-friendly homes out of natural and recycled materials. Conventional construction is part of the polluting, wasteful system that is driving the many global crises, contributing to massive biodiversity loss, climate change, and growing economic inequality. At this time in history, when most buildings are built in unsustainable ways — with materials mined and extracted, creating mass pollution and waste — this is some very important work.

Unlike some ecobuilding initiatives, The Mudgirls' work goes well beyond offering alternative building practices. Teaching, building, and organizing, these women are offering inspiring alternatives to many of the deeply entrenched social inequalities and systems of oppression underlying and driving the social and ecological plights we face: patriarchy, hierarchy, and capitalism. And they don't just confront these forces by saying no to them — they provide a model, a vision, and lived experience of another world: a fundamentally different way for humans to live in harmony with the Earth and in equality with each other.

Our founder, Jen Gobby.

The Mudgirls Natural Building Collective is an all-women group. They empower themselves with skills and employment in a traditionally male-dominated field.

Childcare is built in to all their events, workshops, and meetings; they bring care for the next generation to the front and center of social change and insure that parents have equal access to learning and employment.

The Mudgirls are structured non-hierarchically and practice consensus-based decision-making: challenging top-down, inequitable power structures by practicing ways of working together in which all voices are valued and have equal decision-making power.

They are challenging the capitalist paradigm of business by keeping their wages lower than market value and by practicing bartering systems of exchange.

Through hands-on workshops, they have been training and empowering hundreds of people with skills to build their own homes and their own collectives.

As this book shows, The Mudgirls model a different kind of activism. It's what one friend of the collective calls applied activism. While constructing buildings, The Mudgirls are simultaneously deconstructing capitalism, patriarchy, and inequality. Where some activists focus on educating people about the destructive and unethical impacts of these forces, The Mudgirls provide themselves and others with tangible, hands-on experience and skills based on feminist, collective, non-hierarchical, anti-capitalist principles. The Mudgirls are creating spaces where we can start to unlearn patriarchy. This kind of applied activism is helping us break out of social structures created by capitalist logic, that separate us from each other, from our own labor, and from the land. Instead of arguing that a better world is possible, The Mudgirls are enacting and showing this better world through their building practices, their business model, and through their organizational structure.

While this book has many helpful tips on building techniques, it is focused more on the revolutionary process and practice that this group of women embody. It shares insight and inspiration about starting and sustaining a revolutionary collective, regardless of what work a collective takes on. This book doesn't shy away from identifying the challenges that come with this kind of collective process. We're raised in a culture based on hierarchy and individualism — principles hard to unlearn. Sometimes, collective process can be very difficult!

And I know the challenges of collective process well. I founded The Mudgirls Bartering Collective in 2004. The current wage-earning collective started three years later, and I worked full-time with them until 2010. Being part of The Mudgirls Natural Building Collective was the most empowering experience of my life thus far. Nothing has taught me more about myself than the years I spent as a Mudgirl. I learned how powerful I can be. I discovered in myself an organizer, a teacher, and a leader. I also found out what a control freak I can be, and the collective helped me confront the internalized power hierarchies in myself. Being part of The Mudgirls empowered and challenged some fundamental parts of me. It also raised some huge questions for me about how we can affect larger social change by scaling up the small-scale, locally focussed initiatives like The Mudgirls.

After some unexpected twists and turns in my path, I am now in my final year of a PhD at McGill University in Montreal, working with climate justice activists and organizers in Canada, studying how large-scale social transformation happens and how we can strengthen our movements to be more powerful. From this current vantage point, I look at The Mudgirls Collective with new eyes.

There is amazing work going on, on the streets, on blockades on the land, and in courtrooms. People across Canada and across the world are actively opposing the expansion of the Alberta tar sands and proposed oil and gas pipelines and other extractivist projects that threaten ecological and social well-being and violate the rights of indigenous communities. This is the crucial work of opposing and resisting the capitalist, colonial expansion. Sometimes, though, these movements are criticized for merely saying no. What are they saying yes to?

Groups like The Mudgirls are creating, living, and promoting such alternatives. Their work can serve broader environmental and social justice movements by providing the resistance with inspiration they can point to when people inevitably ask: How do you think we're going to live without fueling our economies on oil and gas? The Mudgirls are showing that there is a low-carbon way to provide ourselves with homes. There are other, non-capitalist ways to make a living. There are other, viable ways to organize ourselves that align with our values. Theirs is such an important niche in the movement ecosystem. The Mudgirls are continually exploring and living the yes. Given how much needs to change in such a short time, we need more projects like this, that manage to foster multiple practical benefits simultaneously.

This kind of activism helps us unlearn what capitalism and patriarchy have done to us. It creates space for transformation in our hearts and minds. This is the kind of activism that helps change the stories that we tell ourselves and each other about what we're capable of. It changes our stories of what activism looks like. This is a kind of social organizing that is resilient, that clearly it isn't dependant on one leader to keep it going. It builds leaders. It builds confidence. And perhaps that, in the end, is my favorite thing about The Mudgirls: it is actively building confidence in the world. I have always loved the look on a woman's face, while helping build a house for the first time, as it dawned on her that she could build her own house. If she could do that, she can do anything! And this sense of renewed confidence in our own ability to transform the world around us is so badly needed in these cynical, doom and gloom, "why bother" days: it is the confidence that the world can be remade. And we can do it. And that we don't have to wait till we're experts, we can do it now.

It is my hope that *Mudgirls Manifesto* will help inspire readers to create their own collectives to do important hands-on work in their local communities in ways that confront the systemic oppressions and systems of domination. There is no one "right" model of collective organization. Each one can and should reflect the local needs and conditions and be designed around the values, concerns, and interests of the collective members. All you need to know is: do the work, do it together, and do it as equals.

Let us know how it goes!

Collective Statement

When we began working as a collective, most of us had very little building experience. We learned to build by building. We hope this book will encourage others not to wait for permission to embark on the building of their dreams, never forgetting to celebrate the things that go right along the way.

An old rusty saw finds a new purpose — trimming the cob walls.

Part I:

A HISTORY WRITTEN IN MUD

Chapter 1:

Our Ways of Building

Guiding Principle #1: We work mostly with unprocessed natural and recycled materials to create and decorate beautiful and healthy structures that are Earth friendly.

Guiding Principle #2 : We believe this work to be so important that we cannot wait until we are all experts. No matter the level of experience, we value each individual for their contribution and abilities and believe strongly in skill building on the worksite.

We Went for It
Creating the World We Wanted to Live In

WHEN THIS WHOLE THING GOT STARTED about 10 years ago, as a group of 20 or so women, we pretty much had no idea what we were doing. Certain members had previous natural building experience — our founder, Jen Gobby, had taken a comprehensive natural building course. Another woman had studied drafting. We also had a carpenter, some herbalists, a baker, a tree sitter, a lawyer, and a circus acrobat. The rest of us were enthusiastic learners, and we all felt compelled to take action. We were a bunch of young women, some of us mothers with babes at the breast, with little money and a few survival skills. We found ourselves fundamentally dissatisfied with the options on offer for addressing our basic needs in a way that lessened

Workshop participants positioning windows in a cob wall.
CREDIT: BRIANNA WALKER

our contribution to the mess we were making in the world, and avoided enslaving us in a exploitative economy based on debt and credit, mortgages and ever-increasing rents. It was real: we needed shelter, and we needed meaningful work. We realized that if we wanted to provide homes for ourselves and our families in a way that made any sense to us, we were going to have to come up with something that didn't exist yet.

The place where we all live and call home is the south coastal region of British Columbia, Canada. This area is a temperate rainforest, very different from the rest of Canada: the winters are much milder and wetter, and our summers are dry but rarely extremely hot. It is a wilder part of the world where large expanses of forest cover islands running north to south, dotted through the sheltered Salish Sea. To the west of these Gulf Islands is Vancouver Island, to the east, the mainland from Vancouver to the Sunshine Coast. People drawn here over the past two centuries have tended to be those looking to find their fortune, whether it be furs, gold, or timber. Beyond economic reasons, people came for the freedom, the wildness, the get-away-from-it-all, close to the land subsistence living. Obviously things have changed, but still people arrive here from faster places, looking to slow down. In the times before chain building supply stores, newcomers made do with what was around them. Here on the BC coast, there is so much to build with. It's brimming with wood, clay, sand, lime, rocks, and resourceful like-minded folks. It's because of this place, because of its bounty, because of its people, that we have been able to walk out and find what we were looking for.

Building things is a very direct route to satisfying basic needs. Natural building was a revelation: a direct connection to materials, innate knowledge, with the laser focus of necessity. We realized that people have always provided themselves with shelter using what was at hand. Having given ourselves the permission to build shelters out of the materials around us, both natural and recycled, we also gave ourselves permission to design our group and our way of working around our needs, instead of around some imagined legitimacy or marketplace.

In essence, our idea was to build homes for each other, and to teach others while we were doing it. We were going to keep the process very affordable so people like ourselves could come, and so we could share the knowledge as quickly as possible. Genius. So simple. So beautiful. This is what Jen Gobby and her partner Pachiel had been doing already at their place — offering workshops that taught people how to build a cob house — her cob house. This is where the women that became The Mudgirls first met — at Jen's ridiculously cheap, ridiculously fun, and inspiring series of workshops.

At the very beginning, we valued our inexperience as an asset to creativity and built it into the way we work and teach. Sharing knowledge and skill building on the worksite has always been integral to the development of the collective. If we waited for everyone to be an expert,

Some satisfied newbie natural home builders, circa 2008.

we would never get this great idea off the ground. This radically simple, fun, beautiful, empowering, new/old way of building was something more people needed to know about, and fast. We knew that what had attracted us would attract others. There were a lot of people like us out there, feeling disillusionment and lack of alternatives. This was turning out to be about way more than providing shelter.

We sought to incorporate the skills each of us already had that didn't necessarily even relate directly to building, because we were going to need way more than just a roof over our heads — the kind of houses we were talking about building weren't going to fly anyplace that was flush with services. We needed to think like pioneers: Where's the water coming from? How were we going to grow food? Will we have electricity? What's that look like? Where were we going to poop?

We sought allies. Our workshops would feature guest speakers from the community, or workshop participants themselves, on things like bike repair, solar power systems, pirate radio, medicinal herbs, homemade micro-hydro turbines, singing, whatever. When you think about it, everybody has some cool useful thing they know that can be shared. We were pooling our resources. We wanted to get a revolution brewing. We shared the belief that there was so much to do and face in the world; change was coming down quick, and we needed to forge communities that could withstand the economic, cultural, environmental, and political stresses that can divide people. In order to be sustainable, we also knew that this group was going to have to be a ton of fun,

because we are people who like to have fun. This collaborative spirit gave us inspiration and support from the earliest days onward — we had each other, a direction, a passion, and even the possibility to create fairly paid work for ourselves so we could sustain this amazing thing we had found. The revolution had begun.

Looking back, it seems kind of amazing. Not just the idea that we were going to build anything, let alone houses, but that we were going to organize this riotous band of impassioned idealists into a thing. We ran workshops where people camped together, ate together, and cared for each others' children, even taking on wet nurse duties sometimes. We built together — teeny tiny spaces and whole houses, ovens, walls, benches. We traveled and met people and were part of their dreams for their lives. We learned more that first season than we could ever have imagined. Not just about building, but about working and living together, the reality and pressure of client expectations, and looking

It's dirty work, and everybody wants to do it! Nobody said we couldn't have fun at the same time.

Workshop participants happily smoosh earth with their bare feet.

after the health of our collective and our families, all while trying to uphold our grand social and environmental vision. It has not always been an easy balance to find, but easy gets boring real quick.

Somewhere in the last ten years, the worry that all the oil in the world was going to run out turned into something a lot more scary. Now we can't just surf the apocalypse by mastering caveman technologies. Climate change threatens to destroy the actual systems that support life on Earth. It threatens entire countries. Climate refugees are a real thing, fleeing rampant fires, back-to-back 100-year floods, landslides that devastate homes, fields, and livestock. We could go on, but you know already. So what are we to do? How will we care for these displaced people? How will we prepare for a completely unpredictable climate, and changing community dynamics? Because you know, it might be us running for our lives one of these days, and we should all hope that someone will look out for us, take us in. We hope that our hearts and minds are ready to roll with this mess we've created without hurting each other more than we already have. The world needs Mudgirls and the resilience we are trying to build into communities, now more than ever.

The Measuring Tape
Skill-Building as a Priority. A Non-intimidating Approach to Building

Who hasn't played in mud before? Somewhere in our ancestral memories, we harbor an innate and wholesome connection to natural building. Once you get your hands working in this reconstituted earth, you feel a surge of understanding, as though you have done this before. Surround yourself with piles of sand, clay, straw, and a hose, and it can seem anything is possible! We can build a wall out of mud; that's a revelation. But there's a lot more to consider! What about the roof, and the digging, and the cutting, and the height and the slope, and the sawing, and the measuring ... and the ack! The variety of tasks can quickly become overwhelming, or worse — boring. Building a wall out of mud with your bare hands is primal and monumental. Thinking about gutter systems ... not so primal. It can help if you remember that it's your building resources and your values that are precious; not the hoops you have to jump through for a building inspector. Water is precious, that's why we're going to figure out how to collect it. Wood is precious, that's why we're going to figure out how not to burn too much of it to stay warm throughout the years. Your life is precious, that's why we're going to build something beautiful with toxin-free, natural materials. When you consider that your house is going to be a big part of your life, your little abode becomes an ecosystem, full of relationships; then insulation doesn't seem so boring anymore. Gutters will have you throwing your head back and laughing like a decadent millionaire as water rockets off your roof and into your cistern. Once you get stoked thinking about gutters, go back to the beginning and just take it one step at a time.

Without the bigger picture, it's easy to get steps out of order and create a new and unnecessary set of puzzles to solve. If you approach a building like an ecosystem, though, the puzzle pieces start talking to each other. Instead of feeling like you are memorizing arbitrary things, imposing solutions, and struggling to keep it all straight, you will feel increasingly like the materials themselves are helping you find solutions and order. Mistakes will be made, but this is where the best learning takes place. Understanding how something could have gone better only comes when you look back on what you have done and see how changing the order, or taking more care in this or that thing, would have made your life so much easier right now. You will feel new knowledge muscling its way into your brain. Be ready for all the new ideas; one of them could be the next best thing since the baling machine!

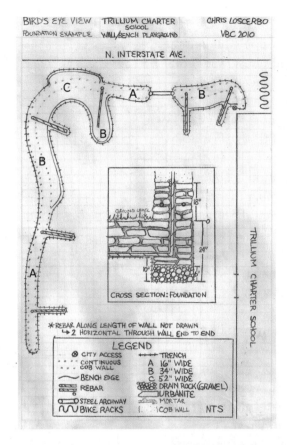

BIRD'S EYE VIEW | TRILLIUM CHARTER SCHOOL | CHRIS LOSCERBO
FOUNDATION EXAMPLE | WALL/BENCH PLAYGROUND | VBC 2010

N. INTERSTATE AVE.

TRILLIUM CHARTER SCHOOL

GROUND LEVEL

18"
24"
10" 6"

CROSS SECTION: FOUNDATION

*REBAR ALONG LENGTH OF WALL NOT DRAWN
↳ 2 HORIZONTAL THROUGH WALL END TO END

LEGEND
- ⊗ CITY ACCESS
- ∙∙∙∙ CONTINUOUS COB WALL
- ⌢ BENCH EDGE
- ▭ REBAR
- ⊏⊐ STEEL ARCHWAY
- ∿ BIKE RACKS
- +++ TRENCH
- A 16" WIDE
- B 34" WIDE
- C 52" WIDE
- DRAIN ROCK (GRAVEL)
- URBANITE
- MORTAR
- COB WALL
- NTS

We can't always go back and fix our mistakes. Patience and problem-solving are your best assets. How well do you cope with a change in the plan, how do you make the best of the new situation you find yourself in? From this point forward, how will you do that thing better? Humans are clever. Give yourself permission to go ahead and do it, read, google, take a workshop, experiment — don't let the unknown stop you. You will never "know it all" anyway, so waiting until you "know enough" is highly specific to the individual. Sometimes you have to recognize when you're just putting obstacles in your own way because you're scared of screwing up. Fair enough — but don't let it stop you.

Be one of those people who does things.

In every work of art something appears that does not previously exist, and so, by default, you work from what you know to what you don't know.

— Ann Hamilton

Above: *A simple but clear hand-drawn building plan with cross-section detail for a cob wall at Trillium Charter School (Portland, 2010 Village Building Convergence).*
CREDIT: AUGUSTE MANN

Right: *Clever little suspended tarp sack, invented by two workshop participants.*

Luckily, we have done a bunch of the mistake making for you! We experienced that gross feeling of being wrong together. We worked out solutions together, and sometimes it felt like our fingers were growing their own brains. It doesn't feel good to have messed up, but it feels amazing to work our way through to the eureka, and have that as a shared moment that further strengthens our bond. These adventures have definitely bolstered our confidence and resilience, but they also keep us grounded.

It's why when we work with clients, we prefer to keep it collaborative, and have them work with us, as opposed to exiling them from their own project by assuming we know everything. The people that live

Molly and Auguste describe how to make a simple frame for a lightly used opening window.

Above: *Kate squishes cob next to her ear and listens to the grating/crunching sounds of a well-proportioned mix of sand and clay. Use all your senses!* CREDIT: BRIANNA WALKER

Below: *Constructing a wattle and daub wall with fresh willow. These walls are light and quick to build, with little to no insulation value. Use sparingly, decoratively, and/or desperately.* CREDIT: BRIANNA WALKER

on the land — who will live in this house — are crucial to the success of the structure because they hold the knowledge and the stories of how the land behaves, where the water gathers, clues that will lead us to clay or sand deposits. It is the clients' priorities and values that will inform how we work and what we build, and maybe if they get into it enough, they won't even need to pay us to finish it, because they will feel empowered to finish their own structure! That's the most rewarding moment for us, because the whole point for us is to spread this knowledge. Plus, it's more fun for both sides, and you keep the learning and sharing opportunities alive when you aren't making like a puffy-chest expert.

Fast, Cheap, and Out of Control

Permits = Limits

Where we live on the south coast of British Columbia, each district has different building and density regulations. Municipal bylaws dictate where, how, when, and with what materials, and, as of recently, who can build something on your own land. These rules make sense when applied to large, impersonal contracting companies that are building for profit in a market where land and houses are commodities. This development=profit paradigm dictates that things are going to get done the cheap and fast way. If left to themselves, for-profit contractors might build less than safe, dry, warm homes in the name of saving costs. The capitalist system and its players thrive on this. In this environment,

The forging of relationships: At the end of a seven-day workshop, one participant decorated another participant's beater car with this lovely artwork and a rearranged Rumi quote.
CREDIT: PHOTO BY BRIANNA WALKER, ART BY BRANDI RAWLUK

rules and building regulations are meant to protect a future buyer from being taken advantage of, or purchasing a lemon. These rules do not take each builder and landowner into consideration, only that developed land is an infinite asset to banks: properties reenter the market and are bought (mortgaged) over and over and over again.[1]

Many of the products required to build homes to code are extremely toxic, their very production carrying a heavy carbon footprint, laying distant lands to waste, and they aren't even the ideal materials in the first place. The building codes are sometimes in place not because they represent best practices or the most suitable materials — they represent a secure chain of production that can be provided consistently and efficiently, so nobody has to strain themselves thinking too hard about what they are building with and why. The thinking is that consistent and cheap materials allow houses to be efficiently stamped with a seal of approval that in turn allows them to be insured, thus protecting

Clare and Alex's load-bearing, off-the-grid cob house.

CREDIT: CLARE KENNY

the buyer. (If only insurance stopped there, and did not also serve as another racket that exploits and puts restrictions on people trying to gain access to land!) In many jurisdictions, to build anything outside conventional building regulations requires an engineer to approve the house designs, which adds a significant extra cost to an already pricey endeavor. Many people are interested in building homes out of more local and natural materials, but are scared away by all the red tape and additional, often unnecessary, expenses.

Using locally sourced, natural, and recycled building materials is much less expensive in terms of your money and planetary resources. Clay is free, sand is cheap, and straw is a by-product from the grain industry. A lack of understanding of the way these systems perform over time, and unfounded concern over maintenance in wet, cold weather, has put the brakes on progressive acceptance of this method of construction, despite the proof of 500+ year-old mud buildings in very wet parts of England and many other ancient earthen structures in Mexico, Japan, Africa, and the Middle East. There are people in the natural building world who are working diligently to bring methodologies like cob into code, and we are so thankful for their efforts. For example, Ann and Gord Baird of Eco-Sense[2] built a beautiful home that people can tour and see for themselves. This home was built with natural building technologies that satisfied all code and seismic requirements. With people like Ann and Gord pushing at that end of the spectrum, our collective doesn't have to feel guilty for looking for ways to buck the system. They have legitimacy covered, so we can merrily continue to provide examples of building things that make sense for people with no money. Not to say we don't often collaborate on projects that are fully code and/or engineer approved — we do so all the time. But what really gets our hearts pumping is figuring out how to do things according to good sense and natural laws, not according to capitalist logic.

> *The market doesn't decide everything. We can decide what's better for people and the planet.*
>
> — Winnie Byanyima, Oxfam International

Earthen materials are breathable; this is one of their key benefits. In mainstream building, a current trend is to create airtight dwellings in the name of energy conservation. Completely wrapped in plastic, they require expensive air circulation units to exchange stale inside air with fresh air from outside. This is necessary because we humans are mostly made of water, and we release quite a bit of moisture through just breathing, let alone cooking and sexy time. If the building we live in can't breathe, moisture will condense on the walls, ceiling, and windows, and the house will begin to come apart at the seams, mold will take over, the home will become unhealthy. Here, on the wet coast, people deal with this issue every winter when hot steamy humans are cooped up inside. So wrap us in plastic, give us vents, and we'll be as happy as a bicycle commuter in a "waterproof yet breathable" raincoat? Yup, sure, for a while. But what happens after that measly ten-year warranty expires, or if the builder was hung over while she taped the seams of your plastic wrap and missed a bit? Soon, there is water seeping under the siding onto the plywood, into the insulation, into the stud frame — and because it's all encased in plastic, it can't dry out. It stays invisibly damp all fall, winter, spring, and boom: you have joined the leaky condo circus, you're under the big top, living the tarp life.

Now, if the *natural builder* was hungover and missed plastering that spot over the window, it can be fixed easily and cheaply, and will be

The beautiful farmstand and pizza oven at Golden Tree Farm, Salt Spring Island: its thick cob walls keep veggies cool, and compel people to slow down for a closer look.

able to dry out evenly with the breeze. The best part about building naturally is that you will have hopefully gleaned all sorts of knowledge from your eager-to-share Mudgirl team, and will be able to take care of the problem yourself without shelling out for expensive, professional fixit labor. Most problems can be seen right away and dealt with promptly. Insidious internal degradation that won't be noticed until months later will be very expensive to repair. Breathability is key to any building's long life.

In practice, our healthy suspicion of building codes has translated into knowing enough to avoid things that will definitely prompt a building inspector to come calling. As it happens, these are things you should do anyway: keep it small, and make sure your neighbors aren't going to give you a hard time about it. Most inspections are complaint driven, and even the most code-perfect house can get held up by someone who thinks your mud hut is ugly. It turns out neighbors are part of natural building! So start getting along.

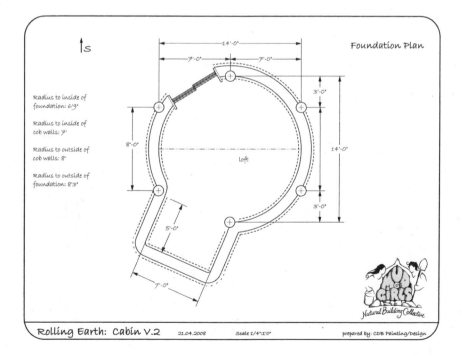

Mudgirl draftsperson Chelsey Braham's simple and clear foundation and post placement plan for a small cob cabin.

Deep in the forest on wee little islands, we have and are building small breathable dwellings. Some have been built with only the permission of the landowners, the workshop participants, and us, of course. Is it possible that such permission is enough? On land owned not in any part by banks, on land the owners have a relationship with, and are planning to die on? Capitalist logic sees land only as a profitable commodity to be developed, sold, and resold. Banks rake in the interest each and every time that piece of land goes through the system. Our freedom to choose how we live our lives is kidnapped, forcibly wrapped up in this plastic capitalist mind-set, and tossed out, regarded as irresponsible and a little bit crazy.

When you decide to build yourself a house with non-conventional materials, using natural building principles, your motives are obviously very different from those of a large contracting company. You are willing to risk guaranteed sales potential in favor of a safe, healthy, enduring home for you and your family. Are you going to cut dangerous corners, are you going to make something that will fall apart before your grandchildren are born? Or are you are going to build well, with thought and consideration for the future of both the land and the people on it? It's in these cases that we believe that building permit bylaws are extremely limiting, in part because they are based on

Participants learn to sculpt designs in plaster and use non-toxic earthen paint to brighten up the exterior finish of this strawbale house in Lillooet, BC (see "Clay Paint Recipes That Work" in Chapter 9).

the assumption that people don't actually want homes, they want "real estate." While we fully realize that the concept of "real estate" is a fact of modern life, it pretty much demarcates a philosophical Great Divide of building things at all. If you're worried about resale values, maybe a house that lasts 600 years is a liability. So once you work that out with yourself, you can proceed to the next order of logic: on your own land, you should be able to submit your designs to the local council, have them deemed structurally sound (if they are), sign something giving you full responsibility for your actions, and be sent merrily on your way. Let them mark your deed with a big red flag if they must, but if your primary concern is not your "real estate's monetary" value, then you should be free to continue building your life. This goes against everything our culture tells us — everybody knows that we're all supposed to "get into the market" — pour everything into a downpayment and mortgage, and hold on for dear life. Hopefully you'll sell it at just the right time and make enough money to do it all over again. It's a lot to ask that everyone should be interested in this deranged gamble. The Mudgirls want to provide a true alternative. We aren't even quite

Small spaces require thoughtful design. This cob house has a custom kitchen built right against the curving cob walls, creating more counter space that you can still reach across.
CREDIT: MOLLY MURPHY

Cheerfully colored clay paints brighten up this old shed that has been retrofitted with natural light clay straw insulation and cob benches. It is now a sweet cozy tearoom.

sure there is one, but we're working on it. This is when it might dawn on a person that a revolution is indeed in order. By releasing people to build their dreams, we're opening up the possibility of grand new innovations that will change the way we live, not just in our homes but in our neighbourhoods, our communities. We can develop precedents that others can reference, and last but not least, we can have the freedom and opportunity to learn from our mistakes.

Messages from Mud
It's Not About How Much You Know, But How Much You Believe in What You're Doing

When you walk into a mud house, you get a distinct feeling. It's relief intertwined with wonder at the forms and textures that surround you. It's ancestral fibers stretching out into modern light and suddenly reminding you of something you had forgotten for a really long time. It's a place that holds you just right, makes you lower your shoulders from your ears and breathe deeply. The air is clean and dry, and you feel calm and sheltered.

Perhaps this sublime impression echoes the empowerments of all the human beings who put their laughter and tears into those walls with each handful of barefoot-mixed earth.

People come from all over the world to participate in the creation of such dwellings with us. And when we are finished, the owner gets to feel all those feels. Maybe the person who has travelled from near or far to help build and to learn doesn't quite see the same picture, at least not at first. They work hard, dig, peel logs, move wheelbarrows donkey-style up steep, root-filled forest paths. They stomp, pull, drag, and carry bucketload after bucketload of homemade mud and place it exactly here it needs to go. Handful by handful. They laugh, play, eat, and make connections over the walls they build. Those connections are woven into the earth just as the straw is, both equally holding the whole structure together. The connections made over the cob wall go forward in time. They continue on in the world after the workshop

We try to tell people to stop laughing and joking around. They are obviously not taking this stuff seriously. The struggle is real, people.
CREDIT: BRIANNA WALKER

is over. As the house is finished, relationships are formed. As those earthen walls go up between people in the material world, they start to crumble in the builders' hearts and minds. We are doing so much more than building a wall higher — we are making our worlds bigger, better, and more alive.

Nydia and Brianna met not long before this picture was taken. Living, eating, working, learning, and laughing together makes for fast friends, tight new bonds that last the workshop and beyond. Credit: Brianna Walker

Case Studies

Ray and Soozie's Place

There is this little island around here where the rules are different — what rules there are, are held up by those that live there. In this small community, a group of twenty-some women coming together deciding they were going to build houses out of trees, rocks and mud, and other people's discarded trash was hard to ignore. Ray and Soozie heard us loud and clear and were interested in a little guest cabin on their land, made entirely from the stuff the island could provide.

   Here in this builder's dreamland, we had no building council telling us how deep to dig, how often to place structural supports, dictate insulation value and chimney distance from the wall. These things are terribly important, of course. Freedom is great, but if the universal laws of building things get overlooked, Very

Ray and Soozie's stunning cob cabin, built in collaboration with many local folks.
CREDIT: AUGUSTE MANN

Inside Ray and Soozie's cob cabin. Bright walls increase the feeling of space.
CREDIT: AUGUSTE MANN

Bad Things can happen. So, being that the newly minted Mudgirls were pretty green at this housebuilding thing, we befriended a few allies. Folks that were not afraid to do things outside the box, folks that understood how a building works, folks that for some reason took us seriously and were happy to be along for the ride, to share their thought, care, skills, and knowledge. The house was built with the inspiration of the landowners, the knowledge and wisdom of long-time island dwellers, and our keen minds and ability to rally folks and organize it all into one complete building plan. With dates set for crew jobs, community work days, and a series of Mudgirl workshops that saw us teaching groups of up to 18 people at a time, this house got finished, and The Mudgirls were effectively launched. Ray and Soozie's cabin is a beautiful standing[3] example of how the power of an idea and the willing cooperation of people can create a thing so precious, one-of-a-kind, that fits exactly into the environment it resides in.

— Mudgirl Molly Murphy

Measure Twice, Think Three Times, Cut Once Because Chainsaws Are Forever

Back in the spring of 2010, we were embarking on the building of a little house in a remote wooded area. We hadn't dug down very far before we hit bedrock in a few places, which meant we couldn't make the entire site nice and level to itself. This left us with a very uneven starting point, but not beyond what we felt we could handle. The design called for three sets of posts. Each set is called a bent, each bent was made up of two cedar posts in the round and one fir beam, all notched and bolted together. The house would have a loft, the loft floor would sit on the beams. The top of the beams that connected each set of posts would need to be at the same final level in the world to insure the floor of the loft would also be level.

If the site is uneven, it just means all the posts need to be different lengths. To make this happen with nothing but wild rocks to help you out for post pads, you need to figure out the final floor height and the loft height, and then you can calculate the differences in the length of the posts, subtracting the post length as you get on higher and higher ground. The higher the ground, the shorter the post. This makes sense after doing it a few times, but can be confusing at first (as you can imagine).

We had one member of the collective skilled in the use of a chainsaw doing the wood cutting as we puzzled out the math. We had readjusted the measurements on one of the posts a few times, and the marks we made were probably getting a bit muddled. Too much was going on at once, and, well, as you can guess, the post was cut too short. In seconds it was over. A tree that we had scouted, taken down, limbed, peeled, and notched was now useless for this house. We had to go into the woods, find another tree that met our criteria, take it down, limb it, peel it, notch it, and assemble the beast one more time.

We learned a lot with this mistake. We realized that so much depends on proper communication, proper understanding of what's happening at all stages of the building. If we had kept our cutter more informed of what was going on, they wouldn't have been so hasty to cut, and we wouldn't have all ended up so annoyed with each other. The awesome thing was that because we were using the materials that immediately surrounded us to build this house, we were able to simply head back out into the landscape and harvest what we needed pretty easily, and with a very low carbon footprint to boot.

— Mudgirl Molly Murphy

Chapter 2:

Women's Work

Guiding Principle: We are a women's collective and seek to empower ourselves with employment and the skills to build homes.

Mudgirl Chris hammers in a spike on a small roundwood structure.

No Boys Allowed

Why We Chose (and Still Choose) An All-woman Crew

WHEN THE MUDGIRLS COLLECTIVE was taking shape, the concept of an all-female crew was largely a means of addressing the gender divide in available paid work on the Gulf Islands. Women were doing underpaid (or unpaid) gardening, home care, cleaning, and childcare, and the men were getting living wages doing all the other jobs. On the islands, "all the other jobs" are about building things, moving things, and digging things. If a couple broke up, sometimes the women would actually have to leave the islands because they were unable to support themselves and their children. We figured that if we learned how to build houses, we'd be addressing two issues, at least — we'd have jobs, and we'd have houses! The challenge — it's not a straightforward thing for girls and women to access those skills. Women generally don't grow up around tools and building things the way that many guys have. Trade schools and construction sites aren't always welcoming to women. Like women before us, we could have gritted our teeth and run that gauntlet of proving ourselves according to someone else's priorities, but we had no interest in perpetuating the values of the economy in general and the practices of the housing industry in particular. (In case we haven't said it already — the housing industry is an incredibly wasteful, environmentally destructive activity that results in energy-sucking toxic boxes that enslave people with mortgages. Boom.) We needed a new way to approach skill-building, and we wanted to put our values into practice, but to do it, we needed to carve out a niche that was ours alone.

We felt some urgency around this — we were a bunch of urbanites and new mothers with no money and few skills. We needed to provide shelter for our families, believing that the world was going to end next year. If this was going to actually happen, we were going to have to enter into a whole new set of relationships with materials, culture, and economics in order to make it happen.

No problem, right?

Ummm ... The Patriarchy

Much like climate change, some people think it doesn't exist. It's a fact that women often have to justify themselves more and fight harder for the spaces they want to occupy, whether it be flying a plane or carrying a stupid rock across the yard. How were we going to disrupt this state of affairs?

Deciding on an all-woman crew effectively hit pause on expectations about what a building site is supposed to look like, and how builders conduct themselves. It created a space that asked the question, "So, this is different ... *How* is it different?" It reminds us that we don't have to follow the rules if they don't make sense. It's a signal, broadcasting that we have given ourselves permission to make this look the way we need it to look. If we're women, we're going to do things in a way that make sense for that reality. We're going to have free childcare, we're going to care for ourselves because we don't just have to be strong for

our job, we also have to be strong for our families. It's not just a metaphor — those hungry babies are going to get breastfed at lunchtime! At the same time, we're assuming that the people who come to our workshops are there because they have the same struggles and questions as we do, so we're going to try to make sense of it all together. We remind ourselves of what worked for us: keeping the learning cheap, the work accessible, and providing free care for the kids. This might limit what kind of clients we attract, but it insures that the clients that choose us understand where we're coming from. Because our values are front and center, we don't find ourselves in situations where we feel disrespected or exploited. So guess what — we love our job!!

Two workshop participants share the heavy load.
CREDIT: BRIANNA WALKER

Mud Mind

Our decision to be a collective of women is intimately bound up in the materials we use. Cob, apart from being breathable, strong, beautiful, and light on the Earth, is incredibly accessible and requires no special tools. The materials themselves have not been commodified and co-opted by the consumer economy — they are cheap or free, and there are no codes dictating how they should be used. The literature we encountered was populated by women who joyfully encouraged an experimental DIY approach. Mud is abundant, forgiving, sculptable, immediate, and real. Building with earth while contemplating how to be lighter on the planet imparts a feeling of direct connection with the primal forces that feed our lives.

So — our newly minted collective didn't need special tools, we didn't need special skills. We didn't have to invest money, nor pay for further schooling or equipment. We could just begin. We could also totally screw up and start over without blowing the budget.

The fact that cob is not part of building codes is relevant: it was much easier for a group of women to become dominant in the field. If there's no big money to be made because the materials and techniques aren't part of the industrial supply chain, let's face it — chances are there's not going to be as many guys around already staking out that space, telling us how it is. Cob building was ours to inhabit and define. The fact that it was necessary to embark on our experimental building projects in more remote places, where the codes were not enforced, was another limiting factor that ended up being an incredible tool of our empowerment. All of this was awesome. Nobody could tell us we were unqualified, because nobody was qualified! Nobody could walk up and kindly offer to operate the chainsaw on our behalf (i.e., disempower us) because we were way in the backwoods of Lasqueti Island, in that amazing forested laboratory of cool, resourceful, supportive people and possibilities! We could learn and share, screw up and haul ass to our heart's content.

Girl Gang

The question of why we are women-only is one half of the equation; "Why are we a group?" is the other. We came into this work with shared questions, concerns, and needs, many of which stemmed directly from our experiences as women. We didn't necessarily recognize some of

Above: *Moving gravel by the bucketload to a remote building site: the Mudgirls don't want to make it look too easy . . .*

Right: *Teamwork is the best way to work.*

those things as women's issues until there was a critical mass of us all trying to function with babies tied to our backs. If there had been only one mother, that mother would have stuck her kid in daycare, and we wouldn't have thought twice about it. That's what the dominant culture tells us to do. Because we were all women, we suddenly noticed what was going on. A group brings in more experience and insight; more complications and solutions; and more support in times of stress. A group is more resilient — it can change, add or lose members and still be the group. A group is also a ton of fun. We bring the skills, but we also bring the ruckus. Having each other to turn to for help and camaraderie is the most amazing thing.

Foremothers

The initial Mudgirl workshops (that Jen Gobby hosted herself on Lasqueti before we formed the collective) were not just about building. We came to her workshops as people that had already come to the conclusion that the economy was about to destroy the world, so we were looking for a true alternative economy that encompassed not just providing shelter, but food, feminism, environmentalism, and community. We brought our stories and experiences and whatever expertise we had in whatever area: farming, herbal technologies, eco-activism, permaculture, music, civil law. We let all this richness inform the collective.

We realized that we had a pretty amazing opportunity to represent something very different from both conventional buildings and building sites. Choosing a women's collective made it easier for us to enshrine and communicate values that are traditionally thought of as more feminine — care for each other, care for children, care for the Earth. On the other hand, we weren't buying into some biological determinism that relegated women to nurturing roles they maybe aren't interested in. Obviously, these are values that everyone should care about, not just women.

There were things we didn't even anticipate until we had already started down this path. Staking out that space had the effect of throwing things into relief that were hard to see otherwise — just because we say we support mothers, doesn't mean the mothers feel supported. Moms in our culture often feel isolated, rooted in an omnipresent "your kid, your problem" philosophy. Unless we dug into this and figured out what it really meant to welcome people who have kids, we were going to miss out on having some amazing women participate in creating a collective. Having free childcare at all of our projects is the most radical thing that we do, and it simply would not have happened if we hadn't been a group of women. Through shared experience, we saw a solution that seemed so counter to the capitalist and patriarchal logic that we were all marinated in, that at first, it seemed ridiculous. Now, it's normal. We want to keep making new normals.

In more ways than we even realized at the time, we effectively side stepped the baggage and bullshit of justifying our skills and our

Mudgirls Melisande and Sheera feed the animals.

existence, by entirely inventing our own arena of work. Surprisingly, a huge part of developing an entity that couldn't be argued with was to declare ourselves a women's collective. Not only were we going to use materials that few people had experience using, we were going to manage projects using a philosophy that we ourselves had developed, and on top of that, we were people that folks didn't associate with building stuff. Nobody could tell us we weren't doing it right, because we were the only ones around doing it. This was very liberating. It allowed us to toss out the rule book and create something that made sense for the lives we wanted to live and the world we wanted for our children. Until we made the fact that we were women *the whole point*, people (including us) might by default still look for the man and defer to the man. We're steeped in our patriarchal culture, men and women alike. It's like a maze sometimes, navigating the assumptions we are lost in. We answer variations on this question regularly: "Why are you women-only?" It continues to make us think. We have discussed including guys over the years, and for the record, we work with guys all the time and have great experiences. It seems to us that we have had great experiences precisely because we are a women's collective, staking out that space and making it clear how we want to operate and be treated.

Our sons just as much as our daughters need to see their mothers building the house they're going to live in. Men need an alternative to macho, hierarchical, dehumanizing construction sites. Women need to experience the camaraderie that comes from building something together. We all need role models and examples of people plain old living their lives right now, as if nobody was standing in their way, as if there were no rules that only served to uphold the Great Derangement.[1] Our collective has created a kind of bubble around itself — a laboratory where we can put ideas into action that wouldn't fly in the "real world." Except that they have. Our social and economic experiments have resulted in actual houses being built for actual families. What it means to be women doing this is hard to put into words, but it means everything. Being strong in our identity has empowered us and allowed us to invent our own game; to trust ourselves. A future where we are Mudbuddies sounds great, because we love and value our male comrades. However, the longer we work together, the more we realize how deep the patriarchal mind-set goes, how much more work there is to do, and how sometimes it even feels precarious, like it could all slide backwards....Women the world over are still treated as property.

Instead of pointing out the myriad ways we find ourselves disempowered by even the most well-meaning people, we choose to present the simple fact that we're in charge, and get down to doing stuff. It's amazing how much clarity this attitude creates. It's not like "Sorry, only the women were available for this one." You can almost hear the "click" of recognition when someone realizes this isn't an accident, or the boss just hasn't shown up yet.

Occupying this space has allowed us to really inhabit the absence — the absence of instinctively deferring to men, instinctively protecting male egos, the absence of all the little things we have become accustomed to letting pass.

We can't uproot all the cultural baggage before we build a revolution. There's no such thing as a clean slate, anyway. We need to be allowed to get on with it, and just like the building materials we choose to use, we'll work with whatever we've got lying around. Unfortunately, what we've got to work with is a culture that isolates mothers by making childcare so unaffordable that it pretty much prevents women from returning to work after having a baby; that values male voices over women's voices; that perpetuates widespread violence and discrimination against women and blames women for that violence; that still refuses to let women make decisions about their own bodies. So what do you do? You get your buddies together, support each other, and live fiercely in the face of bullshit. We meet men and women every day

Mudgirl Rosie at the saw during her internship at O.U.R. Ecovillage.
CREDIT: MINDY SJOGREN

Ryan brandishes the willow they've prepped for a wattle and daub kids' playhouse.

who are forging a better world and welcoming in new thoughts and approaches. We want to be a force that supports those new approaches. There's a lot of crap, but there's so much good. Choosing an all-woman crew feels like a headlong charge through stupidity, like we are creating our own light to see by. Our choice ruptures expectations just enough that we are set free to self-define a space to live and provide examples of women's solidarity, creativity, skill, power, fun, camaraderie, and kickassery.

We Play With Dollies

Work Smarter Not Harder

Let's get some generalizations out of the way. Women in our culture are not supposed to be strong, are not expected to be. People are often surprised or alarmed, and rush to help, when they see women moving heavy things. We often feel we have less to prove when it comes to lifting, pulling, and dragging. We feel less shame in asking for a helping hand, since our culture seems to expect women to need it.

It could be understood that by being smaller, you've got to be smarter — you have to *think* your pile of 20-foot fir beams from the beach to the site. Muscling them (or as we say "manning" them) is just not possible, at least not without many hands, and not the way we as Mudgirls are committed to doing things — with a minimum of reliance on machines. If something big needs moving, we gather our forces, put one person in charge and lift, pull, and push, sometimes from some pretty gnarly locations, into the clear of the building site. We've built rock slings with metal bars and old sheep fencing, dragged logs off the beach up a gravel road on a kayak dolly, pulled wheelbarrows up craggy hillsides with a human tied to the front and another pushing up the back.

We've learned that brute force would not solve too many of our building obstacles. We have had to think about the best way *before* doing it. It wasn't our first instinct — our first instinct was to keep up with the man, even though there often wasn't

Mudgirl Molly at 34 weeks pregnant, rocking the mixing station!

one around — we still felt a need to perform in expected ways. It didn't take long to realize — once we saw the diverse abilities of folks that were attending our workshops — that we had nothing to prove, at least not on the muscular side of things. What we had to prove was that we did things differently. So, we call over and ask four people to help drag the pile of cob closer. On our worksites, we don't want aggro injured heroes. The biggest lesson for us has been that humans are awesome, and we actually love helping each other. It makes you feel good somewhere deep inside yourself. That feeling permeates and becomes addictive, and contagious.

Two women work as a team to pin courses of straw bales together.

Each of us only has this one body this time around. To have it sprained, twisted, and wrecked before the age of 40 in the name of pride, speed, or downright stupidity is not our intention. We're responsible to ourselves and the people who love and need us. So it's crucial to ask for help, and to take a moment to stop and think not just of your next step, but of all the steps that will let you reach your goals. The thought of what might happen down the line helps us tackle unforeseen deviations from a plan. Solutions come easier when you keep the larger picture in your mind. We like to plan ahead for ease, fluidity, safety, and fun at all our builds. But boy, have we screwed up. Yup, walls have fallen, bents tipped, windows broken, fingers crushed, sliced, and generally ruined by caustic lime plaster. Mistakes are there for learning. Not repeating.

The diversity of the materials, the custom and one-offishness of our builds means that each situation will present different obstacles. This has created an environment within our group that breeds true innovation. Though we use our bodies hard during our busy building season, it is our brains and our hearts that get the most thorough workout, and the lessons learned don't get soft in the winter like our leg muscles; they last. The systems we've developed over the years get passed from one brain to the next, making the initial muscular effort last for as long as the information gained is passed on. Our collective muscle memories build resilience and community.

We rely on our bodies too much in the natural building world. This becomes apparent each season when a member or participant twists an ankle, pinches a nerve, or other general wear and tear that comes with aging and misuse. The tenets of permaculture helped show us that

our bodies are our best resource. Our physical capabilities in tandem with our problem-solving skills should be used to their full potential, not squandered or wasted in pursuits that aren't maintaining our ideals or creating safer, more productive working environments. We try to focus on ways that insure the long-term use of these precious resources that will see us through the years. And as our bodies naturally age and we can't lift buckets like we used to, we'll still have something to offer: our knowledge, wisdom, and playfulness.

Learning the basics of building a living roof: by keeping things small, we can cover many aspects of what makes up a structure.

Our Heroines

Other Women that Are Rockin' the Natural Building World and Shattering the Status Quo: Athena Steen, Liz Johndrow, and Becky Bee

Athena Steen started building straw bale homes nearly 20 years ago, helping create and develop some of the concepts and ideas used in straw building today. This natural building pioneer has spent a great deal of her life perfecting the art of clay- and lime-based plasters. As an artist, builder, and author, she has co-written and published many books about straw building, earthen floors, and plastering techniques. She is one of the founding directors of The Canelo Project, a natural building education and research center in Arizona, USA,[2] and a personal hero of ours.

"I always had an inherent desire to design, create and build. Early on, I got a job on a standard construction team building a modern rich house in the foothills of Santa Fe. Horrified at the entire process from the pre-determined, fixed design to the monstrously huge and noisy tools made to man-handle prefabricated, over-sized, overweighted and toxic materials and by guys telling crude and degrading jokes all day long (mostly about women.) There was no question that I, as a woman, would always be relegated to the lowest of jobs and positions. I left after three days.

I have since seen how working with natural materials encourages such a different process and relationship. Each material has its own story to tell and trust. They beg to be touched by hand — many hands, big ones and little ones, many, many times. Naturally forgiving and changeable they allow for an intuitive, "feeling" process instead of a purely "all from the head" one. Building becomes more an art of weaving and sculpting forms and textures into something comfortable to dwell in or beautiful to sit on. It is easy to see how Building Naturally pulls women in. They inherently understand this process. I refuse to build any other way.

When working in Mexico, I repeatedly watched as women mixed mud to massage on straw walls, while barefooted children played all around. As soon as the cement would come out, the men with tools would show up, and the women and children would automatically, every time, disappear. Bring back the mud and, like magnets, there they would be there once again."

— Athena Steen

Earthen Endeavors Natural Building³ and the Nicaragua Pueblo Project — Liz Johndrow

Liz Johndrow is a builder, mother, healer, teacher, traveler, and the founder of the Pueblo Project in Nicaragua where she works with women and children, helping them develop the skills to build their own homes using the natural material beneath their feet. Splitting her time between Central America and the US, she is passionate about sharing her skills.

"I have always enjoyed spaces that bring me in touch with my natural surroundings. I spent my early adult years sitting around fires and living in tents, teepees, and yurts. My first job in the building trade was in my twenties with a women's carpentry crew in New Hampshire, and we built a women's artist retreat. Many years passed as I raised a child and studied massage, herbalism, and midwifery. I was deeply drawn to the healing arts and continued on that path for over 20 years. I then worked at a wilderness school and was exposed to the magic of building with cob. I was always looking for safe, healthy, natural, and affordable housing for me and my son. And I loved when we lived close to earth. So I was thrilled when I began to discover that I could bring a deeper sense of connection with my natural surroundings into my building experience, through my choice of materials and design. I then discovered the added bonus of building with community and focusing on simple and accessible techniques. Since those discoveries, I have been passionately exploring the world of cob, timber frame, straw bale, adobe, earthen and lime plasters, earthen floor systems, and tadelakt. From these learnings and experiences, Earthen Endeavors Natural Building was born. The past several years have taken me further into the role of teacher, facilitator, and instructor. My passion in helping others access and learn these skills continues to grow and evolve to this day. Creating safe and healthy homes that are more aligned with the current resources available, and looking to the projected availability of resources in the future, is an important part of my vision. And I love the creative and artistic possibilities and collaborations that come so readily with this work!

My more recent work in Nicaragua with the women in the northern pueblos has been my most challenging and rewarding work thus far. I am working with several women's collectives and teaching the skills of modernizing the traditional techniques with the materials available in those regions. In these communities, we are considering environmental impact, empowerment, self-awareness, possible employment for women, and societal and environmental resiliency within the communities. I focus on traditional building styles of adobe and taquezal with improved seismic resistant techniques, including aesthetically pleasing creative and modernizing techniques, such as various earthen wall systems, improved earth and lime plasters, sculpting, and linseed oil stabilized earthen floors.

This year I am developing The Nicaragua Pueblo Project. The vision is to develop safe and healthy homes through community action and hands-on learning for local women and youth. The most important goal of this project, aside from the building of needed homes, is creating an atmosphere of learning and sharing, that supports the nurturing of greater self-confidence within the women. And from that the hope of providing a greater opportunity to positively challenge the limitations of living in a male-dominated culture, in order to increase quality of life on several levels, and to pass down import-ant values and belief systems to their children.

I will continue to split my time with working with the communities of Nicaragua and my beloved natural build-ing community in the US."

— Liz Johndrow

Becky Bee's *Cob Builder's Handbook*[4] was the first, and often the go-to book, for emerging natural builders. Becky's love for cob and community runs deep. She loves and appreciates the community-form-ing, people-healing properties of cobbing. Becky is an icon, a natural building warrior, and an eco-friendly living leader. And she makes it all sound so simple...

"I love doing something that makes sense in a world where lots of things don't. Cob is such a woman-friendly, powerful, fun form of creating home. I am delighted to have the Mudgirls carrying on the cob/woman magic in this crazy world. Blessings. The answer to every question about cob and about life is: 'That depends.'

When in doubt, cob."

— Becky Bee

We Love Dudes

And Dudes Love Us

He comes over with a bright, sly look in his eye after a 15-minute talk and slideshow about The Mudgirls, and he asks "So why don't you like men?" Well, some of this has been answered in the sections above. The thing is, we do like men. Our fathers, sons, mates, and best buddies are or will end up being men, and we love them fiercely.

We would not be where we are right now if it had not been for some pretty exceptional men. Men who, instead of telling us The Way Things Are, shared their knowledge and believed in us. If it had not been for Pachiel and Adam on Lasqueti Island, this collective of women might never have gotten off the ground. Pachiel has been building with the

Empowerment for everyone!

forest as his lumber yard since he was very young. He knows what he's doing when it comes to building small, building out of the world around, and dynamite at making things work in ways that will work, but may never have been done exactly that way before. He showed us in his special quiet smiling way how to use trees: how to cut them down and peel them, how to find and split cedar driftwood logs, notch them, and join them. It was his unassuming peaceful manner that made us so keen to listen and follow his instructions. Without him, the epic task of building beautiful structurally sound homes out of nature may have passed us by, been too daunting, leaving us diddling in walls, ovens, and benches for eternity. Adam, on the other hand, is a goofball with an anarchist soul. He got us out there, making a website for us long before things like WordPress existed. Adam was our constant friend as our collective evolved, and an immovable supportive force. He even coined the term Building a Revolution, and walked the talk by doing tons of childcare.

Then, of course, there are our long-suffering partners. At first they scratched their heads and smiled as we galloped off to our first boot-camps and away missions, then they realized that this was a real thing; that the revolution was coming to their living rooms, and was enduring year after year. It was sometimes a challenge to always be supportive, but they came to stand up and cheer as we accomplished amazing feats of organization and changes of space. Many of these awesome men have stepped in as cooks, as childcare providers, and even once or twice, we let them help in the building too.

Who said men can't multitask?

Case Studies

Chris's Contribution

"Yeah, my wife is a builder," I tell the woman at the conference. I can tell she's heard me, and I could just leave it at that, but like a proud parent I have to go on. "But she's a *natural* builder. She builds with earthen materials, like clay and sand and straw bales and rocks and beach logs and things, or recycled stuff like old tires and reclaimed lumber. She works for an awesome collective of women builders from coastal BC called The Mudgirls." I say that last part with emphasis like they are as famous as I think they are and expect the light of recognition to go off in her eyes, because, who believes in the revolution and doesn't know of The Mudgirls, right? "That sounds cool," she says. But I can tell that the awe-inspiring totality of of what they really do is lost on her. "But the work is mostly away from where we live, on the Gulf Islands or Vancouver Island or those other small islands." I'm sort of rambling now. "It's like camp work, a week or two at a time. Sometimes it's great for me because I have a bachelor week, and other times I get about 17 minutes of work done while I'm working on my research papers and chasing the kids for a whole week in the summer with no school or daycare." When I'm done giving the speech, I feel proud for both of us. And it's at these times that I imagine the sound of water rinsing buckets at the end of the day and the sounds of the late afternoon summer forest as the strong sun now slips just below the trees. I imagine the post workday beers and the laughter, and I get a bit nostalgic to be a part of the job. But it's not the work per se that creates the longing; it's the lifestyle of those weeks.

J.K. Gibson-Graham in their book *A Postcapitalist Politics* talk about how the extremely pervasive and embedded idea of capitalism exerts power over us because our attachment to this system, as the only system, has so much to do with our inability to truly imagine an alternative. "If we want other worlds and other economies, how do we make ourselves a condition of possibility for their emergence?"[5] Imagining and reaching for the possibility that things could be different, even little things — like cob in place of concrete, or kids at work with their mothers — are moves toward creating the right conditions for alternatives to emerge. The belief that a different system is possible has always been a driving force within The Mudgirls' philosophy. And they work damn hard to imagine and enact the alternatives so we can see them as viable possibilities.

Just to temper the gushing positivity, being part of these temporary Mudgirl workshop communities is not without its sacrifices. Oh, so you normally have a steaming hot latte and bran muffin as per your morning routine or watch *Law and Order* reruns to wind down at night? Forget it. Instead, there is living in a tent, potentially in the rain; you know those mornings when you try so hard not to even graze the tent wall for fear of complete sleeping bag saturation? And lest we forget the communal sore backs, the eating of foods which you may not normally choose for dinner after a day of physical labor, the compost toilets, the cold bucket/hose showers (or no showers), the lukewarm beers, maybe the crying kid who wakes you up in the middle of the night. With great power comes great sacrifice (to quote Peter Parker aka Spiderman's Uncle Pete while he is passing from this life). But it is always the trifecta of building new skills, showcasing a lifestyle, and helping others imagine the possibility of a new system of working, teaching, and learning that makes me so proud of the Mudgirls and the way they do their work. These are smart, strong, and competent women. They have mad skills when it comes to building. I'm a man who loves what these women do, who they are, and what they believe in and work toward. I can't wait to see what the revolution they are working on will look like when it is in full swing.

I would like to consider myself an honorary member. You know, the way they might give graduate degrees from Harvard to kickass mayors, or gold stars to kids on their chore charts even though the dishwasher is only 42% loaded. I guess I feel that way because I have been a part of this for so long. I've slept in the first-ever cob structure built by The Mudgirls. I know about foundations and roofs, about boots and hats. I know what a froe is (do you know what a froe is?) — and more than that, I know how to split cedar shakes with a froe and an artisanal mallet. I've mixed a few buckets of cob in my day. I've watched some of the children in the group grow from beautiful infants to bubbly eyed toddlers to tweens.

Overall, apart from all the collective pride I have in the group, I love that my wife is a Mudgirl. I love that the car is full of dried clay, the dry smell of busted-up straw, and that my work blazers left in the car have this "rural chic" smell to them at the office. I know now after ten years that shoveling buckets of the freshest, and I mean the freshest, horse manure can constitute a date afternoon. I love that when we drive by a pile of rocks or rubble, I try to distract Amanda-Rae's gaze, lest we get waylaid on our journey and end up pulling over to throw rocks into the back of the car. I love the smile on her face at the end of the week when she walks in the door and drops a muddy backpack and a pile of aromatic laundry on the floor. I know that smile comes from the biological response to using your physical body to do demanding work, learning new and awesome skills, eating well, and watching the thing you are working on change so dramatically. I also know that it lasts for a long time after because of the energy of this group of women who have become more than colleagues and workmates. They are some of her best friends, and many even border on a kind of family. And as a result of this, I know they'd have my back too in a heartbeat. I love that she's the one in our family who works the chainsaw. I'm proud of small experimental sections of plastered walls in our house where new lime plasters or clay paints are tested.

For nearly eight years, the Mudgirls have been a part of my life, and in all honesty, my support for the things I know they will accomplish is unwavering. To genuinely rejoice in the successes of others is one of the greatest feelings I know. These women have earned every bit of it. They truly are building a revolution, and I'm pumped to be involved in any way I can. And plus, talk about name-dropping

Mudgirls husband Chris helps mix some slip.

at the cool eco-parties where the subject of natural building comes up, I get to say that my wife is a Mudgirl and that I know the Mudgirls. That may not sound like much, but for the people who have heard of them, you're going to have to trust me on this, that's a whole lot of street cred.

— Dr. Chris Hergesheimer, Mudgirl husband

Set the Men Free

A few years back, we were commissioned to build a cob bench outside a family drop-in center. We decided to run a workshop to get the community involved. It was awesome. There was a dump truck full of drainage rock, there were moms and kids swarming around, moving piles of dirt, having a blast. One of the dads showed up to drop his kids at the center, and was visibly disturbed by the scene. No surprise there — we were tearing up the familiar good old lawn, after all. However, it immediately became clear that his stress was actually due to the "chaos." He stepped up and started directing the action. It was a community project, and he was part of the community, so we let him occupy the role he had chosen for himself for a few minutes until his intensity made us realize that this poor guy was actually kind of stressed out. And with good reason — as far as he could tell, there was a total power vacuum that he needed to fill, because obviously it was just a bunch of women and children and therefore no plan. We walked up, one of us stuck our hand out to shake his and said firmly, "Hi, we're The Mudgirls, and we're in charge." The relief that seemed to wash over him when he realized he didn't have to be in charge was an epiphany for us. It served as a lesson, a seed. What if we can set the men free by relieving them of the expectation that they have to look after everything?

— Mudgirl Clare Kenny

No, Really, She's Doing It

I needed some excavating done on the land we were intending to build our house on, so I called a few excavator operators to come out and have a look at the site. My husband Chris decided to come along before heading off to work, in Oxford shirt and wingtip shoes. OK, maybe not wingtips, but you get the idea. He's an academic and dresses as such. Me, I'm in my work clothes and boots and have clearly been working in mud.

The excavator operator arrived. I walked out to greet him, introduced myself, shook his hand, introduced my husband and started explaining what we needed done. He's an "older 'good ol' boy" type of man, as many in that trade around here seem to be, and started directing his questions at Chris, who just looked at me and waited for me to answer. This continued until he finally asked Chris if he was the contractor in charge of the building. Chris smiled politely, put his arm around my shoulder and said, "No. She's taking care of it all."

— Mudgirl Amanda-Rae Hergesheimer

Contribution from Todd Turik (One Man Among Many Women)

In September of 2009, I attended my first Mudgirls cob workshop. I have a very clear memory of arriving at the workshop and meeting Molly and a few of the Mudgirls that were in attendance. At some point I was told the other two guys that were accepted for the workshop were not going to make it. While there were some guys involved on the periphery, this meant I was going to be the only guy to attend this workshop. I was maybe a bit nervous, but overall excited and honored. Hopefully I could represent my gender well to some extent, and open the way for other guys to take part in a Mudgirls workshop experience. The Mudgirls workshop was relaxed, and interactions involved considerable laughter and candor. Make no mistake though…there was a willingness to learn and a framework of organized instruction and tutelage by Molly and other experienced Mudgirls. The first day we broke off into groups, and we chose tasks and chores.

The days of the workshop were informative and productive. We seemed to act in a coordinated manner, and there were group gatherings to discuss techniques and skills as well as individual assistance while on the jobsite. The thing about cob is that you have to pull up your sleeves and work it! You have to feel it, use your senses. The Mudgirls' focus on hands-on application right from the get-go was ideal, and the experience and tactile memory that goes into the process begins to set in.

I've grown up in a male-dominated family and am very familiar with DIY construction and building. What I appreciated about the Mudgirl experience was that there was freedom of expression, shared creativity, an appreciation of equality and shared input, as well as mutual respect for what we were doing and who we were as a collective. For my part it felt considerably refreshing compared to having a general sense of loss of voice or being treated like a number, a junior, an apprentice, or whatever. And no job had a gender association with it.

I was glad to be a part of the group. The week progressed and was over all too soon. I stayed on longer and continued with the work where I could be of help.

In the years that followed, there were other Mudgirl workshops: plaster finishing, straw bale, and more. I attended what I could, and I was most proud to be in attendance at a "Boots-On" gathering. This was the inner circle of Mudgirls coming together to go over plans for the upcoming year. I was there to help with the food prep and childminding. Being part of this process was quite an honor for me, and again it took place in a relaxed and warm atmosphere.

Today, as I take on building projects on our very own homestead, I consider what I have learned from the Mudgirls. I, my partner (whom I met at my first Mudgirls workshop), and our child, live in the Kootenays. Despite the distance, I stay in touch with Molly and pass on the odd cobbing question for her.

I continue to be inspired and hopeful when I see postings of the Mudgirl construction achievements both in social media and other media forums. The word is getting out. I appreciate having been given the chance to be a part of this and being able to feel like a member — a real Mudgirl!

Todd is about to get wattled and daubed.

Chapter 3:

Rethinking Work

Guiding Principle: We are a collective that is human friendly: recreating our concepts of work to prioritize respect and care for our hearts, our bodies, and our children while we work together. We create a work environment that nurtures us.

Large and in Charge
The Empowerment Inherent in Working for Oneself

THE POSSIBILITY OF GETTING RICH FAST was not the reason any of us got into all of this. We dove headfirst into this crazy idea because we believed we could, we needed housing, we loved the mud, and we loved sharing the passion we had found for creating things out of the earth with anyone who would listen. As noble as these ideals are, if we were going to forfeit regular paying jobs to give this collective idea a try, we were going to have to find a way to earn some money,

While forming the collective, the discussion topic often came back to the question of what to call ourselves. To call ourselves a business invited a chorus of voices. Different women were at different places in their lives with varying financial needs. We were definitely in no place to form a company. Just the idea of going to get a business number, setting up separate accounts, and being taxed was more than the anarchist underpinnings of the group could fathom. The less outside involvement, the less we hooked ourselves up to the machine, the better. Any sort of government entanglements, official scrutiny or administrative busywork was not why we had shown up in the first place. We just wanted it to be easy and not have to answer to anyone but ourselves and each other!

The idea of referring to ourselves as a collective seemed right. We were a non-hierarchical network of individual natural builders, all having varying skills. Perhaps we felt the need to hide this fact. Perhaps we were feeling that we needed to be something in order to legitimize ourselves, and also to protect ourselves — we needed to preserve the fragile freedom we had found. The more we stayed under the radar, the less risk we'd have to compromise anything. We have often thrown around the concept of becoming a charitable non-profit, in order to seek grants and other initiatives out there. In the end, every time we consider changing, we always come back to the idea that we are a collective. No board of directors. No AGMs. Our collective is really no more than a choice to be there: we show up, we work together. The biggest advantage is that the confines of collectiveness are pretty limitless. As we change, so can the collective. All of us bringing different strengths to the group and gathering confidence from it as well.

We relished the realization that we could all choose when we work, how we work, and most importantly, what we as individuals needed in order to create a healthy (and potentially awesome) working environment. From this idea came our childcare policy, our healthy break times and meals, and our approach to making space for individual needs on the spot.

Mudgirl baby Gretchen stomps her first cob. Gretchzilla!

These things are necessary to getting work done well and cohesively, and the ideas encourage us all to value each other on the worksite — it has definitely contributed to our remarkable longevity as a group. We are more than just wage slaves or replaceable hourly workers.

Supporting women to work in all stages of life, such as during pregnancy and motherhood, is our best example of rethinking work. Expecting everyone to work strictly dictated hours, continuously, regardless of circumstances is not what creates a meaningful working environment. Watching your good friends' two-year-old stomp their first pile of cob super inefficiently with a look of wondrous curiosity, does. The work still gets done and done enthusiastically, with care and attention. The variety brings excitement and creativity to the endeavor and hopefully inspires others to do the same and rethink their ideas of work, wealth, and hierarchy.

> "During the summer of 2013, when my son was six years old, we signed up for two Mudgirls workshops. It was not a hard decision to choose Mudgirls, it was the only experience I found that made space for my son while I learned. As a single mother, this aspect made my participation not only possible but extra pleasurable. Both workshops took place in areas of supreme natural beauty. The camaraderie between participants and teachers was genuine and sweet. In a mere week's time, we developed friendships that have stuck with us still, four years later. I enjoyed the experiences so much that I honestly considered moving to the BC islands to be able to learn more and live near this cohort of amazing women.
>
> One of the aspects that I appreciated most was how The Mudgirls know their stuff so well that through their teaching they instill a faith in oneself that we as women can build! More than that, though, they show up as REAL people. We shared joys and frustrations about life as parents, as partners in relationship, as friends. We worked hard during the day and played hard in the evenings,

sharing with our children like a village, like family. After just one week, I felt a kinship with these women that continues to inspire me, and I'm saving up so that we can bring them to California to teach and build at our intentional community."

— Freeda Alida Burnstad[1]

It's Our Worksite, and We'll Cry If We Want To
Allowing Space for Emotions, Needs, and Limitations on the Worksite

Of all the wacky concepts The Mudgirls have come up with, this is probably the most difficult one to accept on a day-to-day basis on a worksite. Unlearning all the ways things are "supposed" to run in any type of job is harder than it might seem. For example — as much as we all wholeheartedly accept the idea of allowing for space and understanding in the moment, it's inevitable that someone, sometime, is going to get stressed and not express themselves like a zen master. Ten years of getting to know and trust each other helps, but such moments can still be a challenging balance between wanting to meet the client's expectations of work ethic (see unlearning above), "gettin 'er done," and maintaining a compassionate skill-sharing vibe. Sometimes pressure results in an unfiltered snide remark that leaves someone else feeling pretty shitty. One could ignore what happened and just expect it to fade away and hope all involved get over it, or you could endure the sinking feeling of having hurt someone's feelings, or — worst-case scenario, assume they are being a baby and should suck it up and not be so darn sensitive.... Right, so none of these options really promote a healthy working environment in the long term; unfinished business corrodes the trust we've built. Yet, being that we cannot sit around on the client's dollar and talk every little thing out, we often rely a little on the first option with a twist — the person *will* get over it, and may require an apology, but we also try to remember that when one of us is harsh, it's often because we're feeling under pressure, or insecure, and holding perhaps more than our fair share of responsibility to the build and the client. So how should mature adults handle the situation without taking too much time out? Six little words, familiar to petulant children everywhere: "Don't tell me what to do," delivered with cartoon menace. If further therapy is required, "Why don't you tell me what you really think?" is very effective. If it's a really serious offense that threatens to bum the whole crew out, we stand up and silently drop our pants in protest. Try it for yourself next time you feel disempowered. "Don't tell me what to do." It's awesomely silly and effective. Empathy and humor are the keys to acknowledging and getting through these tense situations, until there's an opportunity to address things properly over tea or a beer. Another tool we utilize to create open-heartedness on the worksite is "The Check-in." We try to start our workdays with a brief sharing circle; each saying how we're feeling, acknowledging things that are impacting us for good or bad — wet sleeping bag, barfy baby, good news, anything. We've found that it stimulates self-reflection and empathy when you take a moment to feel what's going on with yourself and with one another. If you take a moment to think about

Workshop participants weave willow in Salt Spring Island's Fulford Valley.

the motivation behind some words or actions, you can usually get a pretty clear picture, and not take things too seriously or personally. Even though we all know each other so much better and have an established collective with guidelines and expectations, we still need these goofy phrases to help smooth out stressful situations, ease the pain of a sharp remark, and help the person under pressure to readjust their thinking by reminding them that we are all here to get things done and have a good time. No one wants to hurt anyone else, but we do it, without thinking sometimes. These phrases are tools to help bring things back down to the fundamental realization and understanding that we are in this together.

Having run many many workshops over the years, we have had just about every kind of person you can imagine on our building sites. Most of course are fully able-bodied, young, enthusiastic people with a mind-set not too far from our own. There have been many exceptions as well. Making space for differently abled people has been an amazing experience not just for us but for other participants. People will sometimes apologize profusely before the workshop even starts, saying they are not sure if they can maintain the level of work expected, due to injury or illness. They show up, and quite often end up the most empowered person at the workshop. Seeing the no-strings-attached help they get and/or pushing themselves beyond the box their injury or illness has placed them in brings them a satisfaction that becomes contagious to the rest of the people who are working, eating, and camping with them. The vibe becomes one of connection and care. This is the kind of thing

Three generations on one pile of cob: Mudgirl Sheera, her mom, and baby Noah.

humans in our screen-addicted society are desperately searching for. And it's important.

Bigger Isn't Always Better
Dealing with the Expectations of Conventional "Efficiency" Versus the Efficiencies of Long-term Learning, Safety, Skill-sharing, and Community-building

It's a beautiful sunny summer day. A workshop is in full swing on a Gulf Island. People are stomping cob, laughing, chatting. People are hauling materials in buckets on and off tarps. From the outside, it looks like so very much work. On the main road, traffic is constant. Lots of people stop to ask what we are up to; they are amazed and excited, their drive to work made more enjoyable. The feedback is so positive, and the information about the materials and the process is shared freely. Yet, almost every single time we are in this mid-workshop bliss, we get "You could do this a lot faster with a concrete mixer or tractor guy." For ten years we have been doing this. Does this guy think he is the first to come up with this brilliant idea? Maybe he does. After hearing this for ten years, we have to remember not to bite this poor guy's head off, chew it up, and spit it out. (He usually genuinely thinks he is making a helpful suggestion.) Patiently, we say yes, we have used

Workshoppers overflow the ramparts of Molly's house.
CREDIT: BRIANNA WALKER

machines. Sometimes when time is short and learning is not the focus, we use mechanical helpers to speed up the mixing process. Rototillers, tractors, these really do make a lot of cob and make it fast. They are also extremely loud, stinky, and wait, you are missing the whole point. If this thing we are building was about how fast it got done, then sure, we would go there every time, use those great tools. But it's not. It is not. It's about the people building something themselves — increasing their human capital. The feeling they

get on day three, when they see that each bit of sand and clay has been integrated by their feet, placed on the walls by their hands. And LOOK! Look at what a group of hardworking, newly experienced builders have accomplished. And they did that by breaking through social norms. Eating, camping, sharing childcare — all while not having to yell over the sound of loud machines. Think for a minute what happens if the power goes out, or if gas is scarce — look at what can be done with just our hands and feet. People talk a lot these days about slow food; this is slow building.[2] We are taking the systematic application of "mechanical time savers" out of the building equation. We allow time and space for connection and believe in the collective power of people. We're not just building a house, we're Building a Revolution.

Here lies the intrinsic value of something created by people directly. When the process is slowed down to the human level, the end product benefits by having eyes and hands watching, feeling, and working toward a common goal.

Baby, I Like It Raw

Maintaining the Connection with Raw Materials and Raw Power

At each workshop, we discuss the principles of natural building: build small, build to your environment, build with your community and build with what you have….

Tiny homes are all the rage these days. And for once, against our rebel mind-set, we agree. Build small. You will save money, stress, and probably your marriage (if you have one). One of the things that is not so great about the tiny home movement (though guided by regulation regarding the structure's permanence) is the use of non-local, highly manufactured and processed, ultra-light materials in their construction.[3] In the first places that The Mudgirls built things, there were no hardware stores, just the dump; no lumber stores, just the forest; no huge plant filled with ten types of aggregate, just a few road cuts and piles of discarded pond diggings. These materials were not ordered online and delivered to the site. The site was on the top of a forested bluff. There was a dirt road at the bottom of the hill, but the house was to be at the top. Everything that was required to bring the house into reality was pulled, dug, cut, peeled, barrowed, or carried up to the house site. This may sound like so much work, but to a few strange folks like us, this sounds like fun, like freedom, like something worth doing. Were we young, strong, and foolish? Maybe. But it was true work; in some part of ourselves, it finally felt like building was a job that needed us. A job from which we could see direct results of our actions. Work that when done found us stronger and smarter — and in front of us was a house for someone to live in. We had done this with very little financial output. Instead, we looked into our west coast environment. Right outside in our direct natural world, we saw trees, sand, clay, rocks, old car windshields, scrap windows — and so many other resources that can be found in a tightly knit supportive community. We relished the beauty, the bounty that our near world held. And so much of this bounty was ourselves, our energy and the energy of all the folks who came out to partake in our first few builds. We wanted to create dwellings that were sculpted out of the landscape that surrounded us. It can be incredibly meaningful to build a home out of what is immediately around it. It demands resourcefulness, thought, and time. You can see it when you look at the finished house. You admire the work it took to create; it blends in and fits both the person who lives there as well as the immediate world around.

Kate vs. wild clay; a hyper-local clay source for a small cob house.
CREDIT: BRIANNA WALKER

Of course our locally made homes also have the eco-bonus of extremely low embodied energy in the materials that make them up. Other than the food eaten to power the people who did the hauling, shovelling, and mixing, there was a bit of gas to get the trees cut, to bring the clay over from the neighbours, that sort of thing. No huge mining operations tearing apart the landscape in "some other place," no toxic particulates in excess being released for these homes. In a conventionally built home, quite a substantial amount of the newly manufactured toxic materials end up in the rubbish bin. Renovations are rarely done with the idea of salvage in mind. Perfectly reusable wood, windows, and doors end up at the dump, and some of it never goes anywhere from there; it sits for millennia. In the natural building world, materials discarded can usually just go into the garden or be reused. By living in the natural wild environment, you are changing it at a fundamental level. We try to have the perspective that we are just rearranging the things around into something that looks, and serves as a home. And when we are all dust and gone, the house will once again become a part of the natural landscape. We give thanks for the allowance to do so and wonder if it makes any difference at all.

First course of cob on a dry stack rock foundation.

Case Studies

Ode to the Old: Hand Tools and Handy Elders

I recently met a woman up near UBC who was getting rid of a garage full of stuff. A garage full of unloved stuff is my favorite thing. I asked her if there might be any old hand tools in there. She said, "Tons. Go crazy. Help yourself!" My eyes lit up. I waded in there and gathered up things beautifully and solidly made — axes, bow saws, chisels, and something I'd been on the lookout for — a froe. I came out with my slightly rusty prize and showed it to her, saying, "These are awesome — they're for splitting cedar shakes." She knew all about that. It turned out that she and her husband used to go through the piles of wood the City of Vancouver dumps on Jericho Beach. They'd look for cedar logs, buck them up, bring them home, and fill their driveway with hand-split shakes. They had replaced their roof twice over in this way.

This example of natural building applied to a modern house in the middle of Vancouver blew my mind. This family used recycled, local materials, zero electricity, and very little fuel to maintain their own roof — a huge expense for most families. They did it themselves, for free. It reminded me that what we have come to define as "natural building" used to be just "building." Not only is there benefit in keeping old things around, there's benefit in keeping your old folks around. Elders possess a ton of skills, knowledge, and lore, and they can pass all that along if we have the ears to hear. Solutions are close at hand if we reach out and find our allies. We don't need to reinvent the wheel or pay expensive specialists when we're lacking confidence or somehow feel like, without even having asked, we aren't allowed to do things ourselves, or that it's hokey to do so.

What do I mean by hand tools? I mean things that don't need to be plugged in, charged up, or filled with gas; things that don't stink, pollute, or make conversation impossible. Noisy saws spinning at high speeds can intimidate and alienate people who haven't used them before. No disrespect to power tools — The Mudgirls use them all the time; power tools can speed things up a lot. That's important sometimes, but speed isn't everything. Hand tools have their own efficiencies; they can allow you to get a job done, especially when you're working somewhere remote without electricity. It's easy to forget that whatever a power tool does, there used to be a hand tool that did that same thing. So, pulling that massive beautiful cedar driftwood off the beach so you can use it for posts is totally possible — you don't have to wait for the chainsaw or the crane to arrive. One of the single most empowering experiences of my life was reducing a monster cedar log to something humans could carry with the help of a couple of friends, a sledgehammer, some wedges, and my noodle arms. (One of the wonderful properties of cedar is that it will handily split along the grain, right down the length of a huge log, with a little encouragement from a series of wedges knocked into the split with a sledgehammer.)

Cedar shakes hewn from beach-harvested old growth, using this froe and handmade mallet.

Aesthetically, hand tools are beautiful; they're intimate; they have stories. Somebody's hand wore this groove here. Somebody cared for it, sharpened it, oiled it, and hung it back on the wall. Tools like these can last forever if cared for properly. They're a pleasure to use, built for bodies to wield. How many of those big, long two-person saws have you seen hanging on a wall with folky paintings on them? It definitely looks super cool up there, but get that lovely thing down and sharpen it — it'll go through a tree so fast...

Measurements are made on posts and beams to create the structure of our roundwood roof support systems. Credit: Brianna Walker

We talk about local food security — if the trucking routes get cut off by an earthquake, our food can no longer be brought to us from far away. What about tool security? If the power goes out and we run out of gas, with hand tools it's alright. We can still fix things, keep warm, and build entire houses if we want to. We have the tools.

— Mudgirl Clare Kenny

Delicious food is the fuel that feeds the revolution!

Soul Food
Nurturing Our Bodies

So, building houses when you're not absolutely sure what you're doing? We obviously felt OK about that. Wrangling 15 children in the backwoods with no recourse to Netflix? We got this. Cooking for twenty-five people with diverse dietary needs on two burners out in the open with no refrigeration and limited access to drinkable water? This one, we felt daunted by. Hungry people are scary, I guess. Gluten-free hungry people with allergies are really scary. And let's face it — the revolution isn't going anywhere unless the people are fueled up and inspired with plentiful, nourishing, yummy food. Lucky for us, Bethany Scott joined the original Mudgirls lineup back in 2007 as our dedicated cook. She had all kinds of experience cooking in all kinds of environments for every kind of diet, and she totally set us up for years to come with invaluable insights into sourcing food and things that make sense when cooking for a mob. The Mudgirls don't all subscribe to a vegan diet by any means, but vegan recipes provide the basis of our cooking, for versatility and simplicity's sake. We add variations on the fly (or on the side) where it makes sense. We buy in bulk as much as possible to keep costs down, trundling sacks of grains, pulses, and oats up and down the coast to workshops. We supplement these basics with local produce. We make sure to have a separate snack box for the kids, otherwise they will get into the fruit, eat one bite of each of your apples, and then leave them in the driveway like a pack of marauding raccoons. Our communal camp-out workshop situations have much in common with any frontline activist activities — when the people show up, priority number one is not actually fighting the power, or in our case building the house — the first order of business is sorting out where everyone is going to poop, what we're going to do with the kids, how we're going to communicate, and where, what, and how we're going to cook. Only then can the magic happen. Bethany has moved on, and we're not scared of cooking anymore. Thanks B! Here's a taste. Multiply amounts as needed, according to how many hungry mudpeople you have.

Smoked Tofu Potato Salad

Serves 6

Salad:

6 medium-sized potatoes, cut into one-inch, bite-sized pieces (any kind but Russets)
1 package of smoked tofu, grated
1 medium carrot, grated
¼ cup toasted sunflower seeds
chopped parsley, for a bit of green garnish

Dressing:

2 tbsp olive oil
2 tbsp apple cider vinegar
1 tsp mustard (preferably Dijon)
2 cloves garlic, finely chopped
salt and pepper to taste

Cook and cool potatoes. Add remaining ingredients. Toss until evenly mixed.

This is a flexible recipe. Amounts (and ingredients) can be adjusted to suit availability and taste. Other protein (egg, crumbled sautéed tempeh, tuna, chicken — just not plain tofu, though) can be substituted for smoked tofu.

Recipe

Bethany's Rice Pudding

This is a great way to use up leftover brown rice.

Serves 8–10

6 cups leftover cooked rice (prefer short grain brown)

1 cup coconut milk
¼ cup solid coconut cream (optional, but yummy)
½ cup chopped dates
½ cup chopped nuts and/or seeds
2 tbsp grated lemon
pinch salt
cinnamon, nutmeg, cardamom to taste

Combine all ingredients. Cook on low heat, until dates are soft.

Add other favorite ingredients, such as raisins, apricots, shredded coconut.

Sweeten to taste with maple syrup.

These workshop kids are right at home... near the desserts.

Coconut Curried Lentils

(adapted from the ExtraVeganZa cookbook[4])

Serves 6

6 green onions
4 tbsp olive oil
2 tsp madras curry powder
1 tsp mustard seeds
½ tsp turmeric
2½ cups red lentils
½ tbsp coarse sea salt, to taste
2 x 14 oz cans coconut milk
½ cup cilantro, finely chopped
3 tbsp lime juice
4 cups water
¾ cup whole cashews

Fry first six ingredients on med-high heat for 5–10 minutes. Stir frequently.

Add next five ingredients, bring to boil, then simmer for 30 minutes. Stir in cashews.

Recipe

Energy Balls

Makes about 20 energy balls

1½ cup raisins soaked in ⅔ cup boiling water
⅔ cup nut butter
½ cup brown rice syrup or date purée
1½ cup chopped almonds
1tsp vanilla
Dash of salt
2 cups chocolate chips, melted
⅛ cup puffed cereal or oats
Coconut for rolling

Combine raisins, nut butter, syrup/puree, nuts, vanilla, and salt.

Mix in chocolate chips and cereal.

Form into balls and roll in coconut. (The mix, not you.)

Chapter 4:

Caring for the Children

Guiding Principle: All our events are child and parent friendly with quality childcare always provided.

Our Kids Are Your Kids
A Better Model for the Greater Good

O NE OF THE MOST REVOLUTIONARY ASPECTS of our collective is this: we offer free, built-in childcare at each and every job we do. On our crew jobs and at our workshops, we provide quality care for Mudgirls', clients', and participants' kids, allowing crew members to work their full day, and allowing parents to immerse themselves in new learning opportunities.

When we first formed the collective, several of us Mudgirls had small children. Creating a way for women to continue to pursue their dreams outside of the home was of paramount importance to us. This freedom, if not denied, is definitely put on hold while women, who choose to, raise their babies. We felt a deep inequality in the way in which women's wages are put under stress when they do decide to work, not to mention the long-term emotional impact of having small babies in daycare Monday to Friday 9–5. In most cases, having a baby is a choice we make; even so, nobody can deny that

Mudgirl Jen Gobby's mom, Brenda, taking on the rigorous work of looking after a wee baby.

the results are costly. When seeking childcare outside of the home, all costs are placed upon the parent.

There are inherent costs in having kids, no getting around that. When women decide to to go back to work, our daily earnings are usually reduced by the cost of childcare; this cost can easily be anywhere from $50 to $80+ per day. The burden of this drastic reduction in wages falls more heavily upon the female population. We believe that this doesn't have to be the only way. As women, as mothers, we shouldn't have to make less money per day than our non-mother counterparts. As skilled members of a budding revolutionary building community, we felt that this was the place in which these paradigms could and should be shifted. But how?

We began this journey knowing that this was not a path that would lead us to rolling in stacks of cash. Straw maybe, but cash, no. The Mudgirls wanted to make decent, livable wages and have our work be affordable to folks who normally would never be able to build a small home. We decided that all our building crews would include a paid childcare person. This position would be paid the same as the other positions. While in agreement about the ethics of our policy, we had our doubts as to whether our prospective clients would agree. Would

These kids don't need much to keep them occupied — some sticks, an old watering can, and each other.

others help shoulder the cost of our childcare, when in most other job situations it would have to be covered by each individual mother or family unit?

Clear in our convictions, we went forward with the plan. Each client would be told about our built-in childcare policy. If they didn't like it or agree with it, then they were not the clients for us. That's it. It felt amazing to value ourselves this way. It felt right. We believed we would find enough like-minded folks out there, maybe folks with kids themselves who would love more than anything to spend more dedicated time building their home than minding their kids. Women in the home are especially empowered by this idea. They know that if the Mudgirls are there, they can participate in the building and learning process,

A little dirt never hurt.

and know their babe is safe in the arms of a friend and never too far off if her boobs are in demand. We're pretty sure there have been a few people at our workshops who were there more for the free childcare than for the mud-building, and that's OK too.

We have, in fact, had little to no resistance to this policy. It has been celebrated by most of our clients, and it enabled many single mothers to attend our building workshops. Women who had thought they had to put their dreams on hold realized they could make them come true, and best of all, their kids could see their mom doing something so much more than parenting.

Take Your Child to Work Day, Every Day

Why Mandatory, Built-in Childcare Makes Sense, and Why It's Not Always Perfect

So, we recognize that women shouldn't make less per hour because they've decided to reenter the workforce by choice or economic necessity. This idea to bring our children along really made sense in those early years for the simple fact that four of us had babes at the breast. Leaving them in care was not really a choice that any of us were willing to make. So it began. Travelling from workshop to crew job, from tent site to outdoor kitchens, to oceans as showers. Bringing our kids along for the incredible adventure that it was. For a few of the smaller kids, being at a Mudgirl build was their first time being cared for by anyone other than their parents. Not to mention the first time the moms in the collective were able to do paid work that was fulfilling, all while knowing their children were safe and being cared for. The kids were learning to rely on other loving adults while the moms learned so much about natural building, that returning to their gooey, clingy, dirty kids was worth it. Most of the time.

Other times, going to work meant having your small baby cry as you leave, only to have them cry when you get back. You spend the entire lunch hour with your child on your breast — they suck it back and fall asleep, you quietly slip your tit back into your shirt, and leave them again, all cuddled up in a pile, and you return to work all full and drained at the same time. As the workday ends, it's back to full-time mothering. Now your snotty-nosed eight-month-old is desperate for your love and affection. All you want is a beer and time spent hanging with the crew around the fire. But now it's time to rinse soiled clothes, feed them, hang with them, wash them, feed them again, then lie in bed with them until they finally fall fast asleep. You never venture out of earshot of your sleeping infant for fear of them waking up in a strange dark tent scared and alone. So you sit with a headlamp and a book listening to the laughter of your mates around a just too distant fire. Then it's the next day, and you do it all over again. Is it worth it? Sometimes no, it's not. Sometimes you wish you could drop your kid off at daycare "like normal people" ... that you had a job that allowed you to go home at night instead of finding yourself in an albeit beautiful rural location, but in a tent too small for you and your kids, scraping oatmeal off your shirt again, and doing the dishes, and doing everything that normally would be tackled by you and your partner. Some days it is overwhelming. Sometimes when your tent is full of kid puke, and it has been raining for days, and the outdoor kitchen is just too outdoors, you throw in the trowel and say enough is enough and head home, wondering what you are doing this all for.

Here's the thing though. Sticking it out is key. Now all those babes are bigger and have become workshop aficionados. They know the drill, they are great campers, they love the freedom of running around, meeting new kids, staying up late around the fire. Going to bed is easy because they are exhausted; mom can wander a little farther because she knows her kids feel safe. These kids who have grown up each summer going to workshops and crew jobs around the southern BC coast have it good: different Mudgirls look after them; they have different kids each week to learn to play with or help care for, all the while fostering special relationships with the other Mudgirls' mutts that they see year in, year out. So although it can be a fine test of a mother's sanity in its beginnings, the long-term effect of growing up living at their mother's worksite as a major part of their lives will be a good one. And so far, all the moms are still reasonably sane.

The Children of the Revolution
Children as Active Members of the Community

Kids these days.... People are always saying this. Kids are harder to teach, they can't concentrate, kids younger and younger are getting diagnosed with clinical depression, ADHD, OCD, and other anxiety disorders. Is it too much screen time? The public school system? Is it too many permissive parents, chemicals in the food, or a combination of many factors? Kids get their signals about what to do, how to act from their primary caregiver, the one they have decided is their main compass point in life. They need to have solid, loving, accountable connection to this person especially while they are small. The current cultural expectation to be financially successful enough to be able to acquire all the modern gadgets and things is what drives some families to the point of requiring two incomes. (This is not always the case of course, often it is purely survival economics that drives this need.) Both parents have to work to provide enough to maintain their decided level of comfort. This can place stress on children who have to be sent to care at an early age. In Canada, once you have a baby, you get maternity leave for 15 weeks, which then turns into paid parental leave for at least another 35, so that either parent can stay at home with their child. This is great if you had a "regular job" for the months before you gave birth, if you didn't, you are out of luck. If you were fortunate enough to be eligible for these benefits, you have one year to eighteen months.[1] Once this is over, your choices are to either live off one income or put the child in care so that the other parent becomes available to work. Too many families are forced into this situation just by the pure economic reality of living where we live. Kids are losing their focus point; the amount of time spent with their main guiding force in life is being greatly reduced. This can lead to kids who are lost, lonely, and are easily lead astray by their peers. Peers do not emit ongoing unconditional love, and that is what kids need more than anything else. Kids who without a moral compass point find themselves flailing, searching, and seriously at risk of long-term emotional trauma.[2]

This separation of kids from parents amounts to a modern societal breakdown, a deep cultural void. It is founded on a complete lack of understanding of the importance of a healthy connected childhood for every child. There is also social pressure to get back into the workforce, to be more than "just a mom." The stigma of staying at home past early childhood is frowned upon; it's seen as wasteful and indulgent. For intelligent, hardworking, driven, adventurous women, parenting at home can also feel like being under house arrest; you watch as your brain is slowly being washed away with every load of dishwater that circles the drain. We want to be good mothers first and foremost, of course. But what does that mean in the year 2018? Do I nurse until my kid is five, do we co-sleep, do I get them on the waiting list for the best preschool, do I make sure they are never sad, do I make sure they never taste failure? How do I pursue my goals and still be there for my children? How do I balance my happiness and my dreams with their needs, and how the hell do I insure I raise human beings that I would want to hang out with, who are not self-centered, entitled brats! These are big questions, and the answers are beyond the breadth of the *Mudgirls Manifesto*.

What we've come to learn through experience is that kids at our workshops are in their natural state; they thrive. Sometimes it takes a day or two for the kids (or the first-time moms) to shake out of their comfort zone, but they come out in the end. Kids love exploration of all kinds; they're sponges absorbing new experiences like a tree to sunlight, clay to water. Kids have the opportunity to discover their capabilities in an environment just beyond their individual parent's watchful gaze, while knowing deeply that mom or dad or whomever is just down the hill at the building site, pursuing something that interests them. This arrangement insures the child's emotional safety at the same time; it makes the kids feel loved, trusted, and guided. And hopefully these experiences create a sense for both parent and child that goes beyond just tolerance but to understanding and acceptance that lasts long after the workshop has ended.

In our collective's experience, children, when allowed to use their primary caregiver as their guide in their early years, learn to trust and rely on that closeness even when not in close physical proximity. Our collective made the decision to include children in our daily pursuit of creating a better world. These kids are working with us to make Places out of the materials under their feet and above their heads, fostering that instinctive desire to be shown a direction in life. What direction will it be? We can only wait and see.

> "I'm eleven years old, and my mom is a Mudgirl. I like my mom being a Mudgirl because we get to hang out with other Mudgirls kids and make new friends plus travel to different workshops throughout the summer.
>
> At workshops we build mini cob houses on pieces of wood, out of real cob. We play on huge sand piles and walk the beaches. It is really great to see different workshops and different buildings in different stages. I really like the other Mudgirls too, because I have known them for a really long time. They are like my second and third moms, and their kids are like my cousins."
>
> — Solomon Hergesheimer, age 11 (Mudgirling since age 1)

Case Studies

How the Inner Child Schooled the Adult Attitude: Youth Facilitation as a Non-parent

We share duties when it comes to jobsite facilitation, cooking for participants, and caring for the children. I used to think it was crucial to come well-prepared with games and activities and structure for each day — but I should have known that I too would learn far more than I would teach. Although I'm not a mother, spending time with so many different children reminds me of the importance of spontaneity and allowing freedom and adventure with new friends. Making the most of whatever materials come to hand — for fort-building and racing little twig rafts on the water or spending long afternoons collecting beach glass treasures to exchange with one another round the campfire in the evening. Routine and schedule is enforced early in a child's develop-ment, with good reason in most cases, but off-the-clock, with access to wild nature, children can safely allow their imagina-tions to guide the activities rather than rely upon a time-based schedule of things-to-do.

Mudgirl Rosie takes care of the most important resource we have, and she does it with style (and superstrength)!

Kids have a naturally inquisitive nature, and so long as we keep them safe, well-fed, and we are always on hand with words of encouragement or comfort, their creativity and indi-viduality can flourish in a new and healthy environment. When not wrangling toddlers and counting heads every ten seconds, taking on the Youth Facilitator position encourages you to find playfulness and innovation in everyday objects. I grew up climbing trees, finding forest dens, and beachcombing. How refreshing to be reminded of the joy in these pursuits. At what point did I forget?

— Mudgirl Rosie Graham

That One Time I Almost Lost Kids and My Mind, and the Silly Play That Saved Us All

My first full Mudgirls workshop experience was in my own community, on the farm in which I lived. I had just given birth to a baby girl a few months before, and my land partners had just had their second child as well. I took on the role we lovingly call Youth Fac, as I was constantly nursing and already taking care of my two-year-old. I had facilitated the Mudgirls' youth at their beginning of the seasonal bootcamp and at a crew job already that same summer, so I felt confident in my ability to juggle the responsibilities of my own two kids and their collective five, three of whom were under five years old.

However, it seemed that Roberts Creek had a bumper crop of kids that year, nearly tripling the total number of kids under my wing. This wonderful little community also loves getting together to make things happen, and so we found ourselves and our workshop a hub of activity. Not only were people stopping by to participate in the building, but there were some who stopped by just to hang out, while others obviously just heard about the awesome free childcare that was happening at Rolling Earth. Luckily for me, we had many volunteers willing to take shifts counting the kids, making sure we didn't lose any, as we lived on the edge of a deep forest where many wild animals lived.

One such beautiful woman was Jen Gobby's mom, Brenda, who graciously spent the week teaching rhymes and songs to the kids. It was this that truly saved me those two weeks. Armed with a bucket of dress-up clothes, a box of scrap material, and a sewing machine, Brenda and I produced the greatest rendition of the song "Animal Fair" that Roberts Creek has ever seen, and we didn't even lose one kid. Well, maybe one. But only for an hour or so.

— Mudgirl Amanda-Rae Hergesheimer

I went to the animal fair (spread hands apart over your head like a banner)

The birds and the beasts were there (flap arms and make claw fingers)

The ol' baboon by the light of the moon (scratch your armpits, slow down as you say moon and shine the moon in the sky)

was combing his auburn hair (decadently comb your hair)

The monkey he got drunk and fell on the elephant's trunk (make

drunk face? And do an elephant trunk arm nose)
The elephant sneezed (achoo!)
And fell on his knees (fall to knees)
And that was the end of the monk(ey).
The monk, the monk, the monk! (jump around and do silly things)

Life After Motherhood

(Reconciling my ideas of self as a mom and a non-mom/builder. How the two came together with the realization that I no longer had babies, I had *kids* and the freedom that allowed me to be both.)

Little baby River helps Sheera plaster faster ….

The dependence of babies came as a shock to me. My first unexpected but much invited child threw me for a loop. I used to be a person who did things, I used

to have a life where I was the primary decision maker. At 26, I thought I was finally ready to deal with whatever parenthood had to throw at me. Ah, the ignorance of youth! I still thought I'd be me. Anyone who tells you so is lying. I was not me. I was tired, lonely, and had no hopes for the future other than maybe having a snooze while the babe snoozed that afternoon. The days were looooong. I remember thinking I was not sure I could get through the hours from 5 to 8 p.m. (8 being the kids' first bedtime, where I would get maybe an hour or two of free time before I was sentenced to bed with my boobs suckled until dawn.) Things were not looking bright.

Time passed, my son grew older, and with that grew my freedom. Once the demand for breast milk decreased and stopped altogether, I could feel my resilience returning. Though I had been part of the collective since he was six months old, I often felt withheld, trapped, and confined by mothering an infant. It sounds harsh, cruel even. It wasn't that I didn't love the guy to the moon and back. I made all the sacrifices a good mother makes. I just lamented the loss of coherent thought, reading a non-fiction book, a good night's rest, being able to do as I pleased. It was not a graceful surrender. That, I learned later, with the next two babes.

So I moved beyond these years and found that I came out the other side different, a change for the better. I had renewed my vows on life, as I had something greater than just myself to live for — I had someone to strive for. There were even times that I could go away without any kids. I was able to enjoy the path of sharing my life with someone else who needed me so much. All that compulsive needing, being the shocker in the beginning, became a reliable tool to help me focus on what was actually important in life.

The ability to be included as an equal member of The Mudgirls Collective, to be invited despite my breeding habits, was paramount in my ability to remain sane during those hard first years. It gave me something other than motherhood to focus on; it showed me I was capable of doing things other than wiping butts and lactating. Lactating besides became a superpower, as there were other small babes that needed a feed, and in sharing that bountiful resource, I was setting other women free to move beyond the confines of motherhood and into the realm of self-care and achievement of personal goals. I had found the place where — instead of a battle between being a professional, successful, intelligent human or being a mom — there was reconciliation, blending, and an acceptance of both simultaneously.

— Mudgirl Molly Murphy

Participant/Mother Contribution

When my son was five and six years old, we attended two workshops with the Mudgirls. They were rich learning holidays for both of us. The workshops were rare opportunities for me to immerse myself in learning new and challenging skills for many long days, while being able to trust that my son was in good company and thriving. For my son, these workshops were some of his first experiences being able to spend long days wandering alone or engaging with a community of people he recently met and could trust to watch out for him. I enjoyed learning to build in the workshops, and I am most grateful to have witnessed how the Mudgirls shape their community and business structures to make it possible for both individuals and families to join in the learning of these valuable skills. As a result, I look for opportunities for this kind of sharing and collaboration when I engage with my community. Thanks, Mudgirls, for this gift.

— Khaira Ledeyo

Chapter 5:

Rethinking "Business"

Guiding Principle: We seek to do our business in a non-capitalist spirit. We keep the cost of natural building affordable by keeping our wages low, offering our workshops for barter, building for low-income people as much as we can.

Ménage à Trois
The Breakdown of Our Workshop Structure

OUR WORKSHOPS ARE VERY POPULAR. They are also very cheap. Sometimes we worry that by pricing our workshops as we do, we're not fully respecting the knowledge and skills that our collective contains. But then we come back to the foundational idea of our three-way barter system. It is really important to us that our clients and our participant learners understand how the money that they pay to participate in a workshop is spent.

We Mudgirls are paid a fixed day rate by the client to facilitate and organize a group of workshop participants to build something. Sometimes it is a small something, like a bench or an oven, sometimes it is a large something, like a home. In return, the clients get something built more frugally by a group of volunteer learners, and those few hired Mudgirls. In other words, the participants are not paying us for the learning they receive — rather, the clients are paying a few Mudgirls to facilitate this pool of laboring learners. The participants' workshop fees go toward the wages of the cook, as well as healthy, nourishing, energizing meals (bought as much as we can from local farms or community-supported agriculture co-ops), snacks, and all the leftovers you can carry the morning after. We, in turn, share our knowledge and skills with participants in exchange for their willingness and ability to work with eagerness, to their full ability, for the entire workshop.

If we are hosting a workshop for one of the Mudgirls, we don't get paid at all. Mudgirls volunteer for other Mudgirls, knowing the favor will come back to us when we need a hand for our own place. For the participants, the arrangement is the same — they only pay for the cook and their meals. This format is drastically different from other building workshops out there, where the participants are paying the facilitators. The landowner makes a profit from free labor, with participants each sometimes paying upwards of $500 a week. We saw flaws in this right away: Even the most seemingly idealistic clients will sometimes justify not only having people pay for the chance to build them a house, but charge extra to put toward a mortgage or administration. Just because people are willing to pay for learning, doesn't mean we should take advantage of them. Why do these clients get a free ride? Why do

A call to arms.

facilitators have to make do with such a varying amount of income — from making almost nothing to making a killing? The participants get the crappiest end of the deal; they work super hard all week *and* pay a bunch of money. Or the opposite can occur: participants might believe they don't have to work hard because they spent $1,000 to be there. You can end up with a workshop full of entitled brats.

The Mudgirls' setup is inclusive to all people regardless of socioeconomic status. We offer affordability to those whose income is lower than the average — like us! These people tend to be the ones that want to "live outside the box" in the first place and are often the ones that flock in droves to our workshops. We welcome their diversity, freedom of life choices, and the fact that the impact our workshops have on their lives will be long-lasting. These participants may actually put the information learned to use — necessity dictates they are self-motivated to go ahead and build something.

This, of course, is not to say that those endowed with a more lubricated cash flow don't put their hands where their heart is, because they do. They so very much do. Many people who come to our workshops are professionals in the real world; they want to make the world a

Did you hear about the Mudgirls workshop? Everyone was in tents.

better place too. They're the ones that forge ahead on the legal possibilities of building differently. They can often afford to pay for permits, engineers, even the builders themselves to see their dreams handmade into reality. Without them there would be fewer workshops to host in the first place.

How Much Is Too Much?
The Quest to Practice Sustainable Idealism

> *You never change things by fighting existing reality. To change something, build a new model that makes the old model obsolete.*
>
> — Buckminster Fuller

Phewf, this is a hard one. There is rent to pay, meetings to attend, mouths to feed, jobs to keep, prestige to be gained. We all want to get ahead, but what does that even look like? Some days the box we call mainstream society has towering sides that you cannot see over into the clear of the wild freedom. This freedom comes from growing your own food, collecting your own medicines, constructing your own house, forging your own tools. A magic behind this freedom is the lack of regulations around using the resources nature provides. Sure there are rules, but rules that make sense, ones driven by the laws of nature. Our collective is trying not be guided solely by capitalism's set of rules. By letting nature govern your basic day-to-day decisions, life takes on an ebb and flow; it sets fair limits on what and how much to harvest and when it's available. You have taken your life into your own hands to a large degree, and delivered it into the arms of The Mother. You have taken out the middlemen, the big-box grocery stores, the agribusiness, the FDA, Big Pharma, the destructive, wasteful, toxic processes involved in building a home in this modern, over-regulated world. Our collective wants to take back the power that we've relinquished, or that has been systematically removed from our once-capable society. In capitalism, power has been entrusted to the hands of the few, the ones that are supposed to understand the whole picture; but over time, their view only gets narrower and more compartmentalized. Their reach of influence starts where they have much to gain, and stops before any meaningful change can take place. They only understand the flow of materials and goods and the monies that are cycled through the systems they oversee.

The Mudgirls want to shed the confines that hold us, but we find ourselves lured in again and again. And we're paralyzed by so many different ways to live outside the box. Do I convert my diesel truck to run on veggie oil, do I buy an electric car, do I bike? Do I eat only vegan, but what about local, what if it's not organic? Do I use recycled windows or splurge for the super energy-efficient top-of-the-line new versions?

Everyone has a different idea about what the box looks like, and as a result, everyone has a different idea about what living outside it means. As people already on the fringe, our collective finds that we are about as far out of the box as you can be without being completely excused from functioning society as we know it. Who is actually willing to move to an extremely rural location, grow food, homeschool, weave, bake, can, butcher, forge, and generally repair and create all the things necessary to live a full life? Sounds like a dream doesn't it? And a whole lot of work. Who decides what those necessary things are? For some, a new iPhone is a must, for others, a seamless greywater system, or the perfect pair of gumboots. But for most of us, necessities manifest in an intricate balance of community, sense of place, and material items that make life run smoother. To what degree do you engage in this consumerist culture and still feel like you are not destroying the planet? How often do you excuse your actions, saying you deserve it because you worked hard or you made this other sacrifice over here, so this little treat is fine? How then do you berate yourself for the indulgence of a new computer, new shoes, new car, new kitchen, new house? As conscious members of the first-world economy, we know our decisions in a big-box store actually cause others real pain and suffering. Sometimes that suffering gets overwhelming, and other times it gets ignored. How are we supposed to function in this world once we begin to realize the truth of how things are made, the true price people pay? Not the price in dollars, but the true cost of the land destroyed to get the materials for that new thing, the terrible cost of the indiscriminate use of children for labor, the unquantifiable cost of climate change destruction and knowing we face a seriously dismal future. We are paving a one-way road for our children that is not a future we ourselves are looking forward to. And still we march on, really just wanting someone to tell us to stop, let us off the wheel, and give us a viable alternative. So far, all that has happened in the last ten years seems like The Great Ignorance: a choice we all make every day to ignore what is going on around us. And it's getting worse, not better. Increased spending on the military, approving the construction of pipelines and dams, when we know that spending money on the war machine only creates more war, and that burning fossil fuels is causing the next greatest extinction since the dinosaurs.

Living consciously and sustainably does mean big change in how our world runs, who runs it, and into whose pocket the excess money flows. We give away our hard-earned cash to these thieves of the Earth, knowingly, and we don't protest; we just keep the wheel turning and wonder if things will ever get better.

Simple and handsome composting toilet throne for those who believe pooping in drinking water is crazy.

It feels overwhelming when the problem seems so large. Building houses out of mud does not seem like a realistic or drastic enough solution, right? What can we do? There is no price tag big enough to write the ransoms paid — in *life* by some, in livelihood by others, and in happiness by even ourselves — when we realize that the new things we bought are actually not making things better. They are just another distraction, distracting us from the whole point: to figure out where we fit into this crazy, out-of-control world. We don't have an answer to this; we just know we are on a path that feels right. We make the decision over and over again to change the world, one bucket at a time.

Who Needs Money When There's Mud Everywhere?

A Low Income Plus Resourcefulness Equals Creative Power

Though the planet feels like it's on the fast track to human extinction, bringing us all slowly to a sad and gruesome end, the reality, despite all the ranting above, is that humans are resourceful, intelligent, and innovative. We have the ability — when we put our minds to the task, when we leave our egos outside the door — to achieve the most wonderful life-altering moments for *other people*. Gardens in ghettos, free meals for homeless, veteran tiny home villages, water protectors, Black Lives Matter, pussy hats: all these things are the new fire, the new heat that has been placed under the asses of the conservative and liberal elite alike. All these common people are speaking up, saying that our voices are not to be ignored, our lives are not worth less. The deeply entrenched disregard for our

Early settler home in Saskatchewan, back when local and sustainable was the only option.

right to speak up and be *heard* is being overthrown by many socioeconomic movements.

It kind of makes natural building seem kind of small, kind of miniscule among these much greater issues. But all life is connected. Anyone who feels empowered, for whatever reason, can go on to find even bigger fish that desperately need a turn in the hot pan. That strength to be free, to stand up for rights — and not just the legal ones, the ones for humane treatment, clean water, shelter. Resistance permeates many subcultures out here, and the fire spreads. Once a fire is lit and the embers combine, there is a force to be reckoned with. The comfortable elite should feel threatened by this. What we are beginning to realize now, thanks to the crazy interconnectedness of the twitter, instagram, and FB world, is that we could all be fighting the same fight. We are all looking for more ways to be happy. One thing is for certain: the more you personally and emotionally provide for yourself, your family, and your community, the better you feel about the work you go out and do every day. When you directly know your actions have greatly improved someone else's life, you come home feeling like a success … even if you have no more money in your pocket than you did before you left, maybe you even have less! But you feel rich! So there it is: The Economy of Kindness. The best part is, that if you end up in debt in a world that looks like this, all you have to do is be generous and/or nice to someone and your debt will be relieved.

Houses, ovens, benches, and more are built on this invisible foundation. People get excited when they see other folks break free of the indebted culture cycle. They get so excited they want to contribute somehow and hope by doing so they'll get flung off the conventional wheel and land at a run alongside those that have already left. Because The Mudgirls are there; we are running right now, and we are going somewhere. You should join us. It's contagious, this helping of others, it is more fulfilling than any all-expense-paid vacation. It's what we humans were put here to do.

When there is no money to provide for any extras in life (as in just your basics are covered or not even), you often become so much more resourceful than your steady-income counterparts. If something

breaks, you actually cannot afford a replacement. So you either fix it or find another way to perform those tasks without that tool. Building a structure with little to no money is liberating, really. The myriad of options has shrunk significantly. It may seem confining at first, but have you ever spent time looking at tile or paint samples and felt like it was way way too overwhelming, all those choices? If you need a sink for the kitchen and you come across one at the dump, you grab it, then you might grab another on a different day … or your junk-piling friend drops one off. Now, it feels like luxury having the choice between two, or even three sinks; they all cost you nothing, and you feel great. You can't afford skilled labor so you pick up a book and read about post

Building Mudgirl Amanda-Rae's studio, one handful of fun at a time.

and beam, or round pole building. You make notes, you learn for chrissakes, your ability to become a better equipped, more resilient person increases inversely to the amount of money you have. (Put another way, the more money you have, the less you are forced to learn.) This may be why natural building and Mudgirl workshops are so popular in these tumultuous times: they take a bite out of the need to be extremely wealthy to be able to afford to build something for yourself. They add into your tool belt the ability to think for yourself and solve your problems creatively. When you see what can be done with a little bit of hands-on learning, a reference book or two, other people's discarded trash, clay and sand from the Earth, and the best tool of all — your community, you find yourself wondering what took you so long to get here.

Client-friends and Friend-clients
Keeping a Healthy Building Relationship Without Contracts

Considering our alternative ways of doing just about everything, we have definitely attracted certain types of people as clients. They are, as a generalization of course, farmers, and/or homesteaders of above-average income. Yet they are grounded people who take our ideals to heart. Most of them have worked with the conventional building industry at some point and find our affordability, communication, and approachability very refreshing. We have worked for people who have, up until the point of hearing of us and meeting with us, had terrible experiences with the people they have hired to build their dreams. They have been overcharged, underappreciated, and completely had their own desires and design preferences ignored.

This is especially true when working for a middle-aged or older female client; having come from a different generation, these women can have a hard time asserting themselves in a way that is heard by middle-aged men who "know better." The thing is that in the natural building world these "men of great experience" have actually *not* done exactly this before.

Natural building, by definition, is never the same twice. The realities of the site's landscape and ecosystems, the budget, and the philosophy

and aesthetics of the owner-builder will all inform location, size, what the walls are made of, and how everything will look and fit together. Meeting with your Mudgirl coordinator for the first time can be a revelation for some people. After a few minutes, you see the relief in their faces: relief that this won't cost too much, that their ideas are listened to and incorporated as much as it is safe and physically possible. These new clients are given a time and price estimate based on that; we want them to feel a sense of well-being and confidence that they and The Mudgirls are in this together. When a natural building project faces challenges, we hope to work *together* with the client to resolve them. If plaster cracks, or arches fall, or windows break, or that door idea won't work, these issues will be tackled as a team, with our years of

Penelope lays pebble tiles at each entrance before the top layer of her earthen floor is laid.

experience facilitating the process, and the client's vision incorporated and implemented as much as is possible. We are hoping to leave that first meeting with people feeling empowered again: this project is their build, their money, their dreams. We are there to facilitate with them and have fun while doing it.

The fact that we Mudgirls are all accountable to each other is a great insurance policy for our clients. The MG coordinator cannot just not show up, or take the retainer and flee to the tropics; they can't take advantage of the client without great defamation of the Mudgirl name. This is because of the Guiding Principles that have been at the head of each chapter you have read so far. All Mudgirls are bound by them as a group. In not following through on a part of a job or having a less than good reputation from the perspective of a client, we are letting each other down and not just tarnishing our individual names but The Mudgirls' name. That name represents revolutionary ideals and social and environmental values we have worked hard to maintain.

Building the Revolution one bucket at a time (not a cult, really).

As an example: Su Grout, a favorite client of ours who has moved on to the cozy cob house in the sky, once said, "I don't need to go on holidays every year — I just have the Mudgirls come to my house."

Case Studies

Molly's House

I am one of the lucky ones. Living the dream on a beautiful Canadian Gulf Island. I was already lucky just being here, but things got unbelievably better the winter of 2008. I was at a crossroads in life. I had moved on from the relationship with my son's father, and at the time, I had only my MG income to support me. It being mostly summer work and pretty skint and low paying at that, there was never any savings for the wintertime. I floated around for a few months house-sitting here and there. I knew that this was not a long-term solution as I had a small boy who I felt needed a place to call home.

I did not have many options. There was basically two choices: I could get some full-time job on the island here, put my son into full-time care, and then find a way-overpriced, zero-security rental to live in. This was exactly the trap I was trying to avoid. The other choice was a bit more unrealistic. I wanted to find an alternative that did not close so many doors. I didn't want to send my kid away, nor did I want to limit my ability to do seasonal MG work by taking on a "regular" job.

One day, with thoughts of homelessness looming, I was driving along with a fellow MG, and I said out loud, "There has got to be someone on this island who has land and a little too much money and is willing to let a no-bullshit person like me build a small home. I have the know-how (haha), I have the access to the free labor that being a MG provides, and I don't suck." The next day (I'm not kidding), I was minding my own business at a local cafe when an old acquaintance asked if he could join me. Enter Mr. Harry Warner. Here was a local character, a man who had bought into the housing market before it was completely insane and out of reach for regular people. A man who I quickly remembered had a few rundown shacks that could be a possible landing

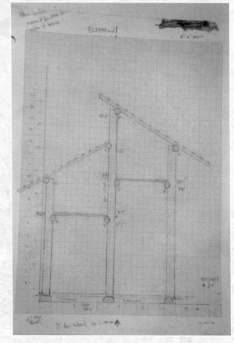

Simple elevation drawing for Mudgirl Molly's cob house.

point for me as I searched out my forever home. A few minutes into the conversation, Harry learns about what I do and believes me about what I can do (which is actually pretty amazing), and in under an hour, we were shaking hands. I would be able to stay in one of the run-down shacks as of February 1st. I would be able to build a tiny home for me and my son. I would provide the labor and host the workshops; he would foot the materials bill, which we were planning on making the smallest we possibly could. I would live there for starters for five years at a fixed rent of a whopping $125 per month. This would include water, shared phone line, and rudimentary power. I jumped on Harry's offer like a squirrel on a lost nut after a long cold winter. All of a sudden, it was real, I was doing it. I went straight to the drawing board, drew up some plans that would carry me and my son well into the next stages of our lives.

On that day, Harry and I never signed a thing. We saw the genuine compatibility in each other and the simplicity of the arrangement. We trusted each other. And it worked; it is still working. Now nine years later, I have a new man and two other stinker cuties to warm our lives. Our house is twice the size now, and we are cozy. Sometimes I want to trade it all in and find a regular life. A regular house that has regular things like closets and spare rooms. But I do reality checks on that greener grass pretty often, and when I get weirded out by my unconventional

From paper into reality: completed dry stack foundation and post and beam skeletal structure to support and brace the cob walls.

CREDIT: BRIANNA WALKER

Mr. Arthur surveys the beginnings of the house his mom built.

CREDIT: BRIANNA WALKER

house and life and dream of drywall and paved driveways, I suck it up and attest to whining about my first-world problems. I give my head a vigorous shake and realize that we are the ones living the dream. And it is good.

— Mudgirl Molly Murphy

Trade Ya a Small House for a Website?

Adam Enright made The Mudgirls a website for free way back in 2007, when it was not an easy DIY thing. We were lucky to have this talented graphic designer launch us from the backwoods into the internet, and open his home and heart to us. We also made him do a lot of childcare.... In exchange, we built him a little cabin.

Wattle and clogs!

> "The first time I heard about the Mudgirls as a concept was over cups of tea and a warm stovepipe in a candlelit, off-the-grid cabin with my friend Jen Gobby.
>
> "And where do I plug in, Jen? I'm not a woman, or a builder," I asked.
>
> "Well, we need a website. If you make the collective a website, we'll figure out some sort of trade."
>
> Thus started an informal arrangement that became a fantastic adventure. The website was created over many late nights of fun, candles, tea, and laughter. The Mudgirls never complained when I went a little too far with creative experimentation. Surprising, because I felt completely unrestrained.
>
> In 2007, The Mudgirls decided to pay me back by building me a cob cabin. It was a dream come true to have an

After two workshops, two weeks of post and beam and foundation work: upcycled tire roof, wattle and daub upper-story walls for speedy lightweight structure and looming move-in date. Gotta beat the rains . . .

Adam's cordwood and cob house on Lasqueti Island.

opportunity to live in a natural building myself. I was not expecting to be gifted such a huge project, but here I was, with the most exciting adventure ahead of me. They gave me a materials list, and Jen and I made road trips collecting windows and doors from salvage shops. Each trip entailed lots of laughs and fun. This is what building a home should be like, no? We strapped secondhand windows to the roofs of old clunker cars, tying them down with scraps of rope and cushioning them with old rags. Then we laughed and sang songs and made jokes as we hauled our finds through the woods and up mossy bluffs. The vision was for a small cottage with a little loft, big enough for a reclusive web designer and a small, scruffy terrier. We took multiple trips with a borrowed pickup truck to dig and haul dozens of loads of sand and clay. Each trip was a workout. Sometimes we'd head out to do a sand run but would end up at the bar or at the beach. Every day was a new adventure.

The post and beam work was a massive undertaking. We took down trees, peeled them, erected megalithic posts, lifted huge beams and bolted them into place. The roof was made with hand-split cedar shakes, and Jen, Auggie, and I spent weeks up on that roof, working and joking and sharing. We'd usually have a beat-up old radio on a cheesy classic rock station. In June of 2007, we had our first workshop. A huge group of people came, half of which were seasoned and amazing Mudgirls core members. They are all extremely fun to be around on their own; put them together, and you have a near riot! It is hard to encapsulate in words the giddy euphoria created when you combine the deep splendor of the woods with jovial intimacy, camaraderie, vision, extremely hard work, exhaustion, and our natural tendency to want to foment a tribal kinship when working voluntarily together on a big project.

The house I was living in became a daycare, Mudgirl Emily's house became the workshop kitchen, a meeting room, as well as a hangout place. Dozens of Lasquetians came to help, and dozens of others came to visit. Food and tea were made in huge pots, and people came together in a buzz of excitement and inspiration.

I'd retire each night to my little cottage with Leonard the Terrier, feeling both incredibly supported and honored, and needing to really process deeply the day's events in the candlelight.

The idea of The Mudgirls Natural Building Collective was revolutionary from the start, what I'd like to call *applied activism*. The Mudgirls go full circle from inspiration, theory, concepts, and communication to coordination, instruction, skills sharing, and hard, dirty, muddy work, to accomplishment! They get houses built. The things they build are infused with love, passion, and laughter. These buildings are healthy and affordable, and built with great spirit and cheer.

This was not "signed the petition" activism, or "showed up at the meeting" or "showed up at the protest" or even "handed out leaflets in the rain" activism. The Mudgirls are "Hand me that shovel let's get something done!" activists. Their activism is manifest in beautiful, amazing, affordable structures. In a world where many non-profits are top-heavy bureaucratic machines with high administration costs producing shiny brochures, the Mudgirls are about action. Each project is an adventure, in new places with greenhorn workshop participants and clients who have new challenges to overcome *together*. New skills to share. New friendships to form, new allies to make. The Mudgirls are building a Revolution!

We are programmed to relate to housing as so expensive — the largest purchase of our lifetimes, something that takes decades of hard work to pay for. And for a growing percentage, having your own housing is an unattainable dream, a dream so expensive it is completely alien. Home ownership has become an economic Unicorn. Our modern ways of living are disempowering and compartmentalizing. The Mudgirls aim to re-empower us to envision our own strength, to build our own homes, not to rely on experts, costly contractors, the banks, government, corporations, and landlords.

I'd venture that the quiet, hardworking, industrious, and challenging environment of the BC backwoods helped The Mudgirls idea coalesce. Lasqueti, like many rural communities, is small and tight-knit; it encourages hard work, self-motivated ingenuity, and skills sharing. If something is broken, it's up to you to try to fix it. If you've never done it, now is a good time to start. Necessity drives you. There are always neighbors who are willing to instruct you or lend a hand. It is this creativity and strength of character that rubs off quickly on newcomers.

I'm so happy to see each and every year new projects launch The Mudgirls to even more new fun places, and new people have joined that I have not even met yet. But I know this revolution will continue to grow and evolve."

— Adam Enright

Chapter 6:

Who's the Boss?

Guiding Principle: We are structured non-hierarchically. Each member is equally valued and has equal say in decision-making.

Guiding Principle: We use the teachings of Compassionate Communication[1] to create a peaceful, mutually respectful, and revolutionarily harmonious group process.

The Internal Workings of The Mudgirls
How We Make Decisions

SECRET: The Mudgirls only spend ⅔ of our time together building things. The rest of the time, we are in meetings. We have meetings huddled around bonfires, sitting on beaches, crammed into Molly's kitchen, by candlelight with headlamps on, under trees, and in hot tubs. Meetings are our favorite thing, and meetings make us want to die, sometimes. We all agree though — we definitely would not have the high level of trust, cohesivity, resilience, and butt cramps that we have, if it weren't for the value we place on committed communication.

As a collective, the members of The Mudgirls meet twice a year. Once at the beginning of the season (Boots-On Camp), and once at the end (Boots-Off). These camps usually last four to five days, and we take turns hosting them. The daily Boots Camp schedule really has not changed much since the first one on Lasqueti Island in April 2007:

We work on a project that is hopefully skill building/refining in the mornings, and meet to discuss policy, jobs, and any other issues in the afternoons.

That first bootcamp in 2007 was a real doozy of a meeting. We had 22 Mudgirls in attendance. All we knew was that we wanted to build things out of natural materials, we wanted the process to be mother-friendly, we didn't want anyone in charge, we wanted to have fun, and get paid. How much money, how to make decisions, how to get jobs, how to stay safe, how to include children, how to not have complete chaos on the building site due to lack of leadership, how to hold all our ideals in check, these were all things that needed to be ironed out in this first ten days together! Jen Gobby had some great ideas coming out of her experience running her own workshops, which gave us a place to start.

The first thing to tackle was how to make decisions. Anyone who has experienced group decision-making knows that even in a room where nobody is senior to anyone else, there are invisible hierarchies and alliances that form. The most gregarious or charismatic or loudest voices are hard to resist. Nobody wants to be the uncool bummer person. We needed to find a way to insure that the people who weren't accustomed to using their voices would still be heard, and we needed a way to create a sense of responsibility to the process that was about making the best decision, not just about keeping the peace and not rocking the boat.

We took the plunge and threw away the option of having consensus minus one; this means that we all have to agree to every aspect of every proposal that is presented. We chose this because we were trying to foster a group of cohesivity, not one of individual egos and lobbying. It was our job as members to have an open mind to all ideas and ways in which to solve any problems that arose. In practice, consensus alone wasn't going to achieve this. Crucial supports for the consensus process for us have been the Circle, Roberts Rules of Order, if you can believe it, and the discipline of Nonviolent Communication. The circle is just that — sitting in a circle. You're facing each other, you can't hide in the back, your hearts are turned toward one another. We go around the circle, and we each speak. No cutting people off or direct reactive outbursts — we're going to actually listen, we're not going to be afraid of each other's views or try to silence each other. Not as easy as it sounds, until you get the hang of not reacting.

Cut back to the first bootcamp in 2007 and 22 strangers, pretty much, sitting in a circle for a ten-day decision-making bonanza .... It wasn't easy! We didn't really know each other, some of us were loud and used to getting lots of airtime, and some of us were more introspective. There were long evenings where meetings seemed to drag on and on. It felt tortuous and the urge to stand up and say "Alright! This is how it's gonna go!" was sometimes overwhelming. Patience and good meeting facilitation always resulted in solutions far superior to any one person's ideas.

We were lucky to have Amber Hieb at that first gathering; Amber knew how to run a meeting, Roberts Rules of Order-style. She showed us how to keep things on track with an agenda, a facilitator, a time-keeper, and a minutes-taker. We still do it exactly like that for every meeting, even if there are only six of us.

A meeting looks something like this: We sit in a circle-ish shape, have a check-in to share how we're feeling, how our winter/summer went, and what level of commitment we can offer for the following season. We usually already have an agenda set up, but topics can be added at any time. We appoint a meeting facilitator — they make sure we stay on topic, talk in turn, and help bring ideas closer toward proposals. The other meeting roles include a minutes-taker, timekeeper, and vibes-watcher. The first two are self-explanatory, but the vibes-watcher was our own innovation. This person keeps a lookout and notices when someone hasn't spoken for awhile and makes sure that they have a chance to; they also watch for someone feeling put off or offended by another member's rebuttal or off-hand remark. This is a very important role, especially when there are 22 people sitting in that circle, as it was that first year. As our membership dwindled and we got to know each other much better, we felt much more comfortable speaking our minds and were less intimidated by each other. We felt safe in each other's company. Consensus has been very liberating for us. You lose the fear that someone is going to veto your favorite idea, because there's no such thing as a veto. We can eventually make whatever it is work for everybody, and it's going to feel so good when we reach that breakthrough. It really is possible, and it's so heart-opening. The oft-heard complaint about this kind of decision-making is that it takes way longer. Over time, we have found the opposite to be true. It's far more efficient to make a decision that everyone likes in the first place, than to push something through that not everyone is comfortable with. The festering resentments and divisions that result from not listening to everyone mean you're just going to have to do it again down the line anyway, with way more bitterness piled on. Pushing decisions through isn't just inefficient — it erodes the very foundations of the group that you've put your heart and soul into. Just like with building anything, take your time and do it right.

At that first meeting, we came up with a Mission Statement and a few Guiding Principles, most of which open the chapters in this book. Stating these principles was probably the most important thing we have ever done as a group. It connected us all, it has kept us focused on why we got involved in the first place. We can refer to them for guidance, and they allow nonmembers to see into the real shift The Mudgirls are trying to make in building, social organization, and interactions with our surroundings. Our Guiding Principles make us proud, keep us humble, and knit us together in a way that brings deep deep satisfaction in our lives. They also help give newer members a frame in which to bring their ideals and inspirations into the group.

Don't Tell Me What to Do

A much scarier hurdle for us to overcome was that of on-the-job hierarchy. We would not look like capable builders if we sat around in a circle discussing every time we needed to make a simple decision, like where to pile the sifted manure, or what order in which to approach the work. The daunting part was just how would this fit into our framework of non-hierarchy? How do we have some sense of organization and display competence on the job without resorting to having one person boss everyone around. Most of us have been rebelling against authority since adolescence, so being bossed around is not an easy thing for our

egos to let slide. Working well together comes down to trust in the end, but that trust takes time and experience to develop. It comes when you learn enough about someone that you can let them make the calls, that you yourself do not always have the right answer. Or it comes when you have asked a crew member for advice on how the top of the wall is going to weirdly go into those rafters; even though you are supposed to be "in charge" and therefore know every-freakin' thing, you get a non-patronizing, carefully thought-out suggestion, one that you can use without feeling like you are losing something. There's no shame in seeking advice or another perspective. Knowing which person to ask and when is a sign of quality leadership; blunt-headed perseverance despite great resistance is not.

Overall, the hierarchy dilemma was actually easier to solve than we thought. This paradigm of one person in charge is the general norm

Mudgirls build a funky shingle roof over a cob wall.

in our society. So, it was expected from a client's perspective to have one person who looks and acts like they are the boss. But from The Mudgirls' perspective, "the boss" is just the coordinator of that particular job, like an expedition leader. It is important to distinguish the words "leader" and "boss." There tends to be an order in which things should be completed to get the most efficient and highest-quality results. Designating one person to hold those details and make any final calls on how things should go allows for a smooth workflow and happy co-workers and clients.

Shared leadership is a trade-off — it doesn't necessarily mean the best decisions will always be made (as anyone knows who has worked within a hierarchy), but the compromise makes certain we don't constantly run into conflict on the worksite. Shared leadership also encourages all crew members to make more effort to understand the

Mudgirls take the mud for a spin.

bigger picture, and to give constructive feedback at check-ins or over beers. This way, any coordinator aka "leader" isn't put in the position of barking orders — nobody wants to be that person.

Compassion goes both ways in the temporary sort of hierarchy we practice. We seek to fill the need for new language and practices, new examples of organizing. If you look up the opposite of "hierarchy," you get words like "mayhem." Really? Does our culture really believe that unless someone is Overlord, people won't know how to act? We know this is ridiculous. This assumption is part of what we're challenging.

We do not have many rules to maintain membership. Actually, we have a saying — "Once a Mudgirl Always a Mudgirl" — and that's true in almost every case. Certainly there have been members that have moved on, joined the circus, pursued PhDs, attended law school, and plenty of other amazing and fulfilling paths. The only criteria we do have is that, once you are a member and you would like to work, you must show up to the entire bootcamp that precedes the season you would like to take part in. This makes sure that any MG who has taken a hiatus can reform connections and get up to date on any major or minor changes to collective policy and decision-making.

Mycorrhiza

A Symbiosis Inspired by Nature Keeps the Collective Rollin'

Our world is full of threads of matter that are constantly weaving themselves together, and before long, unravelling, only to be rewoven differently through time. We humans are only just beginning to understand how a slight change in one area can affect things in a seemingly unrelated system. The best example of this is the effect our changing climate has on so many aspects of the natural world — so many aspects that we cannot quantify them or begin to predict consequences. Such is the interdependence of the living systems on this planet with all other geological and energetic systems. There is no real way to separate distinct independent events.

This is our collective. A true understanding of non-hierarchy. As the spider feeds on fly, the bird on the spider ... and the unending circle of resources being reused and recycled over and over. No one thing is more important than any other. Each piece in its place, helps to provide nourishment, shelter, and/or safety in the real world. To embrace this connection, to value it to a point beyond the personal ego allows for cohesion and trust in one another. We have found natural limits to be transformative and reassuring.

Behind the workshops and the crew jobs, there are a few important roles that must be fulfilled for the collective to run smoothly. We have roles like crack watcher (who insures issues and loose ends on our MG forum are dealt with — and also points out those who are in dire need of a belt), email answerer, NVC (nonviolent communication) support crew, and a few others. We call these roles or jobs *the mycorrhiza*, to reflect our interdependence and symbiosis.

Our collective thrives when we divide the work and switch it up regularly so that we all get the experience and the workload is distributed in a way that allows us to focus on the work at hand while knowing other aspects of organization are being taken care of. No one person feels overly burdened by their position or contrarily has access to too

Workshop participants show off their muscles at the end of a hard week of building.
CREDIT: BRIANNA WALKER

much power over the others. We are all accountable to each other. If one of us was to lose the respect of a client or was to facilitate a workshop while not giving it their best, then the whole suffers, and our credibility goes down. We'd get less work, and fissures could arise between our members, leading to discord and dysfunction.

It seemed like the obvious inspiration, nature. As builders who pride themselves on appreciating the true value of the natural world, it is instinctive to look to it for nature's guidance for our internal structure. As a major guiding force, so far it has lead to nothing but compassion, trust, understanding, and a more than a bit of fun.

Case Studies

The Voice of Dissent, and How We Hate to Love It

I remember being at one of our first meetings. There were quite a few women in the room. We are going around, letting people talk, working things out, all the while getting closer and closer to something that would work for everyone. I have a tendency to want to move on, to say things are good enough, to just agree and be done with it. I remember more than one occasion when the proposal for a new policy would be presented after an hour of discussion. We were almost there … then That Person puts up their hand to say, "Wait … I don't agree with that last part …" and the room noticeably withers. We were so close! But being a full consensus group means we have to work through That Person's comments, going around until we find something that works for everyone.

Sometimes it can be frustrating for sure, but when we do find the solution that meets everyone's needs, we all feel so much better. Because we made the decision knowing no one was left behind; we had accounted for everyone's values. Policies generated like this will be that much more solid and sustainable, and won't have to be "enforced." If everyone got along all the time, nothing would ever change. It's adversity that challenges us, makes us use our big brains to find solutions in life. When that coincides with making the world a better place, it's a welcome bonus and is why being part of this collective is so fulfilling.

— Mudgirl Molly Murphy

A Model of Our (Ideal) Steps to Resolve Conflict

We are a group of strong-minded and strong-willed women, each with our own ideas and thoughts about the best way to do things, each with unique ways of seeing the world and feeling the world around us. What does this mean? It means that sometimes, even after all this time and with all the love and respect we have for each other, we do not communicate well.

Sometimes the day's frustration or life's challenges get caught up in our work and our interactions, and we disagree with each other. Worse, sometimes we disagree with each other and keep it to ourselves, trying to brush it off, but at times conflict can boil up and that is when problems arise. And sometimes we need help to really communicate what we have going on.

When these times arise, and especially during the early years, we have relied on the formula of compassionate communication, also known as nonviolent communication. This process relies on empathy and honest self-expression, holding ourselves to our highest integrity and being honest with ourselves, even when we don't know who it is we are, what it is we are doing, what we want, or where we are going. At these times, we also know and understand that no one can do their best all of the time, but we're all striving to do just that. In essence, we listen to each other speak, and try to see each situation from the other person's point of view. This form of communication requires us to have a deep respect for each other and ourselves, even and maybe especially through our mistakes, all the while being vulnerable with each other and the true underlying belief that we can work it out, and we deserve to.

Having each member of the collective understand the process of compassionate communication makes the process easier, and when the situation calls for it, an unbiased member can sit in on a debriefing and help mediate a situation between Mudgirls. Often there are tears and hugs, sometimes including even clients and participants, until everyone is able to speak their thoughts and feelings and feel heard.

Although we have dropped the rigid formula of compassionate communication formally during our twice-annual meetings, being emotionally responsible, truthful, and vulnerable with each other for so long has helped create an intimacy and bond among us that is so powerful, strong, and true.

— Mudgirl Amanda-Rae Hergesheimer

Chapter 7:

Building a Revolution

Guiding Principle: We work together to create this collective as we go, nurturing the creative and inventive and courageously open to the process of transformation.

WHEN SEEN FROM THE PERSPECTIVE of the mainstream media, the world we live in is very scary. From climate change to poverty, war, and all the general nastiness that is perceived on the outside, we can forget to look closely at our immediate surroundings. We insulate ourselves from the community that exists around us because the onslaught of information seems too big, so unknown that its "badness" is unstoppable. We might ignore the best tool that we have to offer: US.

Build It and They Will Come
The Search for Other Ways of Living

Our workshops, more than the individual structures that we build, are what has made The Mudgirls who we are now. The gathering of people from all over the world — from all age groups, genders, and economic backgrounds — enriches and distinguishes each workshop experience from the others. What all these people have in common is a drive to find something better: an alternative not just to building, but to living, connecting, learning, and sharing.

The temptation to "leave it all behind," "to get out of the rat race" stems from the race never seeming to have a foreseeable ending. The

Workshop participant uses a simple earthen plaster to sculpt a honeycomb, complete with little bees made out of old tiles.

CREDIT: BRIANNA WALKER

wheel keeps going around, everything repeats, and life begins to feel hopeless. There is a surge of people looking up from this mundane cycle and seeing that there are alternatives to the capitalist economy, the 40-hour work week, debt, industrial-scale food production, and the current way we approach the building of our homes and community spaces.

What if it was *our business* to figure out what our new role in society was going to be? There are small and large shifts that can be made to create momentum in this movement. The larger the shift, the faster the momentum, but small movements are more realistic, easier to connect to, the goals are achievable, and we can feel the direct results in our communities. Small efforts latch onto your soul — you take a piece of what you experienced with you, carrying it and sharing it. For movements to be sustainable, people need to feel personally connected to the things at stake. You won't defend what you don't love. If we want to feel supported in our communities and by the natural systems that make life on Earth possible at all, we ourselves must generate that love, forge those connections, and fight for them.

The old paradigm (to finish post-secondary education, find a career, and be happy) is a thing of the past. This general mind-set still has many young people thinking that "good job = good money = happy" is where success in life resides. But year after year, young people are graduating with hard-won degrees and monstrous debt. If there are no real job prospects in their chosen field, they are obliged to get any job they can so they can tackle the debt. Trapped in this dirty cycle, the happiness part of their operative equation is pushed into the distant future. Many of the people who attend MG workshops are young people who either have ended up in the education-debt cycle or narrowly avoided it. These people are actively seeking something different: a way out. For some, being thrown together in a group of 20-some strangers, their kids, dogs, and habits stretches their comfort bubble.

And therein lies its awesomeness! These participants see a light through the mess and push themselves into a new community. They let go a little bit of the fear of the unknown in hopes of finding a gentler way to live, a kinder way to interact and in the process learn something outside of the generally valued bank of knowledge. From doing this, they leave empowered and a little braver and little less scared of strangers, ready to make more and more changes. And when they do go back to their lives, hopefully they begin to redefine their roles in their immediate community, family, and society as a whole. A spark ignited in their bellies for change.

What we hope to achieve through hosting these workshops and building things together is that people will come out from behind that hard shell most of us put on every day to ride public transit or stand in line at the bank. Once we have stepped out of our comfort zone and see how easy it is to be ourselves, somehow, just a bit, we don't go all the way back into that shell. From here, we can get out easier, our faces are more open, and maybe our personal walls will fall altogether; we'll see that guy bopping to tunes on his device, and you'll give him a thumbs-up, and he'll smile (and then, in turn, his shell softens a bit). Because even though we know those are real people out there, we forget sometimes. If we want to see change, to find the world a kinder, healthier place, we need to start with ourselves. You've heard it before, but what else is there to say: Be the change. Build the revolution one interaction at a time.

> "I love that my experiences with The Mudgirls have taught me the basic foundation skills and understanding of how to build a beautiful and creative natural home, hand sculpted from the stuff that Mother Earth gives freely. But what really stuck with me were the values embedded in this work: honor, truth, community, collaboration."
>
> — Kari Gunderson, keen workshop participant

Righteously tossing straw in clay slip before stuffing it into a wall cavity.

Don't Muddy the Waters
Trying to Live by Example

One of the things that creates a sense of integrity at our builds and workshops is that we walk the walk. Most of the members of The Mudgirl Collective live what most would call a crazy hippie tree-huggin' witch coven-like lifestyle ... well, maybe not quite all of the above. We each have different levels of what creates comfort in our lives — hot water, flush toilet, garden space....Whatever fancy schmancy conveniences we have in our homes, in most definable ways we have left the common form of living in the Western world. Sure, some of us are still paying off student loans (doh!), and those that own vehicles pay for gas and insurance. To drop out completely has even been tried by a few Mudgirls of yore. The current group of us are living in a way that seems to foster the development of the collective as a whole — being already outside the box has allowed for us to make decisions not solely based on the financials, but to account for more of the personals. These decisions are reflected in how the collective runs, how we communicate with each other, and is why the Idea of The Mudgirls is so much more than the actual people who make up the membership at any given moment in time. Over these ten years The Mudgirls Collective has been in action, we have begun to really, for real, live our dreams, not all of us in "natural homes" but all of us living closer to the land, creating income from places that create excitement in our hearts and stimulate our minds — and, of course, sometimes at least, pays the bills.

We have been asked on numerous occasions by production companies to participate in reality TV shows. At first, we were interested to find out what would be involved in such an endeavor (so excited were we to spread our ideals). After a few emails, we got the picture that a "reality" program would be more watchable and interesting if we took on roles, created drama here and there, good builder, bad builder kinda stuff. Disappointed but not surprised, we declined. We don't need 15 minutes of fame if messing with our integrity was the only way we were going to get it. Along the way, there has been enough tension, misunderstanding, and grief caused by a lack of communication and egos, that bringing up any of it for the sake of better television seemed like a quick way to end all we had worked hard for. It goes so against our principles that it was a no brainer to say "thanks, but no thanks."

> "In a world of common frailties, The Mudgirls stand apart as heroes of their own stories. Common threads that carry over from art to life, demonstrated by example. The cob cannot be rushed. The cob must grow straight and true. That which is not necessary may be cut away. Lessons, learned through dirty hands, can be lived through action. Patience, fidelity, adaptability, and many more qualities speak to a way of life as much as a practiced skill. Hand-sculpted homes, and hand-crafted lives."
>
> — Steven Funk — our hero:
> magical childcare provider and mover of mud

Penelope's earthen floor on Gabriola Island.

Case Studies

Our Collective's Babies: Mudmob in Australia and The Good Earth Builders.

Somehow, throughout my travels, I stumbled across The Mudgirls. It may have been the most influential experience of my life until that point. Attending a workshop with these empowering women was an uplifting process. Creating a home out of materials from underfoot, learning these ancient techniques, and harnessing the power and energy of friends and loved ones to build something from the ground up was an incredible experience.

I got it right from the beginning. It was only the second day of the workshop, and I'd caught myself (in front of Molly) instructing a fellow workshop participant the correct method to apply cob. Molly saw it and smiled; I was a bit embarrassed, and then my life changed.

I knew I was hooked. I would never get the dirt out from under my fingernails again. My dilemma was "Do I become a Mudgirl in BC?" or "Do I return to Australia to spread the word?" In Tasmania, Mudmob was born. I set out to create a similar thing that Mudgirls had going on. I learned from experimental building for myself and others. I undertook a makeshift straw bale apprenticeship that lasted for two years. I worked tirelessly for other owner builders in the state, started running workshops, did a Natural Building Certificate 4 at TAFE in New Zealand, took on professional jobs with other accredited builders, and designed and implemented education programs in Steiner and mainstream schools throughout the country.

During this period of time, I experienced many different types of workplaces. The majority of tradespeople that I come across on larger jobsites would take a moment to realize that I'm actually serious, that I do know what's going on, and that I'm really good at what I do. My years working as a landscape gardener prior to becoming a builder prepared me for working in a male-dominated industry, and I felt that I could hold myself and my ground when need be. Over the years, I have created fantastic working relationships with a variety of professional builders, and I continue to work with them today.

I originally intended to create a collective as I had experienced through Mudgirls. I really loved how much it empowered everyone, including women with children. Unfortunately Mudmob has still not arrived at that place. For years I managed to hold it up by myself, creating a presence as one of Australia's first grassroots natural building organizations, but without enough support behind me, this wasn't something I could sustain for long. I am now a mother, and although I still manage to do creative building projects, I would really like to see Mudmob evolve more into the collective that it was meant to be. Together we can make it easier for everyone, including mothers, to continue working in the trade.

It is happening; there are large projects starting that Mudmob will be involved in. Other female builders, including Bec (an original Mudgirl member) as well as other women who have been touched by building with natural materials, will be teaming up with some fantastic builders to create a new hemp ecovillage in New South Wales. I will be forever grateful for my experience and shift in consciousness. Together we will build the revolution!

— Kate Ogden, founder of the Mudmob

The Good Earth Builders

Almost ten years ago, in the summer of 2008, I attended my first Mudgirls workshop on a tiny little island tucked away on the Salish Sea. (Funnily enough, this detail would one day find its way into my sister's novel, where a magical crone hides away in her little cob hut growing herbs and healing neighbors.) I had been interested in cob building for years but was, at that point, in the midst of having and raising my babies. The Mudgirls workshop was the only one out there that was affordable, since they valued participants' labor as part of the cost, and they provided childcare. Before even arriving on the island, these two details made me aware that The Mudgirls were doing something special, something different, something revolutionary. The other big factor for me, at the time, was that The Mudgirls were a collective of women working together to build homes while sharing their knowledge and skills. For a myriad of reasons, the freedom to learn these traditionally masculine skills from these women felt safe. That speaks to my own history, my own experiences, and how I had weathered them up to that point in my life; this workshop for women put on by women offered a kind of freedom for me to learn something that I had always known I had an interest and a natural talent for but had maybe been intimidated to explore.

On the water taxi ride home from the workshop, my friend and I were so inspired by what we had experienced that we wanted to start something in our own community on the Sunshine Coast. We talked to Jen and Molly and told them our plans to create a similar collective of local women and men to support the sharing of skills and the building of affordable natural homes. They were excited and supportive, and so The Good Earth Builders were born. The Mudgirls were always there to answer questions and give advice. Not long after forming our collective of local women and a token man, an opportunity arose to truly mentor with the Mudgirls. A local group wanted a building on their land, and the Mudgirls were hired to put on a number of workshops. The Good Earth Builders were invited to participate and shadow the MG. We were a part of the process from beginning to end. The MGs shared everything with us from their Mission Statement, Guiding Principles, and WoManual to the gritty details of working through onsite challenges and personality clashes. After these workshops were completed, the MG were always a phone call or email away to answer any questions we had with projects we were working on. Their knowledge has been passed on through our collective to many other members of our community. One clump of clay after another, community by community that they inspire, the MG are building a more than just dwelling, they are building the revolution.

— Michelle Wesanko, cofounder of The Good Earth Builders

Part II:

THANKS TIPS!
(PRACTICAL BUILDING MATTERS)

Chapter 8:

Materials and Tools

Clay Sourcing Tips

CLAY IS ALMOST EVERYWHERE. For the most part, it is formed by the chemical breakdown of rocks, primarily limestone, feldspar, granite, and shale. The clay might stay right where those breakdown events happened until you come across it. When a deposit is more substantial, it has most likely been transported and deposited over time to lower-lying areas, or old river, lake and sea bottoms. This second geological phenomenon is what you are looking for. You want to find where nature left a big, juicy deposit of clay subsoil.

Clay holds water. There is a *big* hint here. Where around you is there standing water during heavy/consistent rains? Where are the water-loving plants? Around here on the wet coast, plants like skunk cabbage, cattails, and sedges are telltale signs that the soil has low permeability. This may mean you have either super clay-rich topsoil (which is no good for building) and/or you have a clay-rich subsoil preventing that water from draining through and away. The latter is what you will dig down to, scoop out a sample, and begin testing.

Once you find something promising, it's a good idea to dig in a few places, at different depths. Look for changes in the color and texture of the subsoil you are revealing. Clay deposits are not always consistent. One might be great for the first 12 inches, and then change into something much less desirable. Whenever you are harvesting wild clays, you must always be looking for these changes. Our experience has told us that if the clay is thick and closer to pure, you will have a large section of it over a significant area. The depth will also be fairly consistent over that particular deposit. If you imagine that this spot was probably an old lake or pond, and that clay was deposited there over the ages, this conclusion makes sense.

If you do not have clay on your property or are unable to to excavate there, you can look around in your community. You can put an ad on your local exchange or the equivalent. You can call excavating companies, and landscapers that dig ponds. If the project is small, you can call your local potters to see if they have bins of scrap clay in their back room. They are often happy to let you have it for free if you swap them some empty buckets. Your best bet to find quality clay in your area is to seek out any folks who have built a natural home; find out if their source has been extinguished. These people are usually very helpful and excited for you, and they will probably be a great resource throughout your project.

The most important thing here is to make sure you go check out the source before you have it delivered or even say you are going to pick it up. Silt can look and act like clay in many deceiving ways. Especially to someone who does not understand what its future use will be.

Clay is smooth, sticky, and plastic. Silt is smooth, sticks to itself when its wet, yet is slippery and crumbly when dry. Silt is really just super small, round sand particles, whereas clay is actually chemically different, electrically charged, and flat, like a plate.

The most common place we have harvested clay is from farmers. They have excess land, they have dug a pond or two, and the piles of discarded pond diggings are usually just hilled up somewhere along an old road access. They also tend to know what real clay is. Excavator drivers can have anywhere from one to 40+ years experience — the old-timers will know what they are talking about, but less experienced operators might just be trying to offload their dump run on you.

How to Test Your Clay
Feel Tests

None of the following *feel tests* are foolproof. The moisture content of the material really has an effect on how these tests perform. Make the test sample's moisture content as close to modelling clay as you can; this will help. And though these tests are not totally accurate, they do give you a feel for the stuff and will help you as you test different samples.

Worm Test

Roll the sample into a worm about ½-inch thick. Try and bend it around your finger. Decent clay will handle this bend with little to no cracking.

Slap Test

Take a golf-ball-sized piece of your sample. Slap it into a pancake on your hand, so it sticks. You should be able to hold your hand vertically and open and close your hand a few times before it falls off.

Non-feel Tests

Jar Test

This is the best way to test clay. Get a one-quart or one-litre jar with lid, a marking pen, and a timer (optional). Fill the jar no more than ⅔ full of your sample. If the material is wet and clumpy and won't dissolve readily into water, you can do one of two things: (a) dry it out, then step on it until its powdered or (b) put it in the water and mix it with your hand until it is all melted into the liquid. Just don't fill your jar too full of water before you hand mix it. You can always add more water later on. Leave about an inch or two of air space in the jar, put the lid on tight, and *shake*!

Shake the jar for a full minute. Find a stable level place to put your test jar down that won't need to be moved for a week. Once you set the jar down, start counting with your marking pen in hand. Count to seven. Draw a line on the jar at the top level of any sediment already visible on the bottom. This is your usable sand content. (We generally ignore this unless it is above 15%. We are testing for clay not sand.) The next thing to fall out of suspension will be fine sands and silts. We give these 20 minutes.

If the silt is over 30%, we generally think it is a subpar sample to build with. This does depend on what you are doing with the found clay.

For plasters or floors, sandy/silty clay is dreamy, but for cob wall-building, it can be dangerous. Silt can act like clay in all ways except its ability to hold things together. See "Why Cob Walls Fall" in Chapter 10.

At the 20-minute mark, draw another line on the jar. Everything that falls out of suspension after this is clay. To get a clear reading, wait at least 24 hours; but if the water is still quite cloudy, wait longer. Clay particles take a looong time to fall, so if the water clears in an hour, find a better source. In most cases, this last layer — the clay — will be a different color and obvious to the eye.

Overall we are looking for a 60+% or more clay in our samples because we want to be able to add the right amount of the right kind of sand to create good, strong building material.

Brick Test

This test is best once you have found some decent clay and you want to determine what the specific mix is going to be for cob walls or other structural applications. Cob wants to be around 75–80% sand and 15–20% clay. So once you know what your clay sample contains, you can start doing some simple math.

Say that our subsoil sample has 80% clay content. Add one part subsoil to one part sand; that equals 40% clay, still too high. Always keep the clay to one part and amend with sand.

Try two parts sand to one part clay; that is approximately 25%, still a bit high. Try three to one; that's 20%, that's better; it could still be too high, but might just be perfect. So do another one at four to one.

Out of each of these mixes make a small brick and place it on a board to dry. You can trace around them with marking pen or find a twig exactly the same length as each brick. This will tell you if any brick has shrunk once it dries. Any shrinkage in your brick means you need to add more sand. A brick that's too crumbly means too much sand. Try a variety of mixes. Include one that you know will be too clayey and one that will be too sandy. This teaches you heaps about what wrong looks and feels like. When they are dry, rub them, try and break them.

Test Panels

This test is great to get plaster and floor mixes and/or colors just about right. (We like to get our mix right first — and then test colors after, because different ingredients can change the final hue.) Figure out how many different variations of the materials you are going to prepare. For the sake of science, try to change only one thing at a time. You are basically going to be making large tiles; these tiles need a frame or mold to hold the wet mud in place while it dries. The frames should be about twelve inches square and about ½-inch deep. Find some plywood scraps for the bottom and find other thin pieces of wood to make the frames. Make your mixes, spread into frames. And most importantly *label each square*. Don't make notes on some random piece of paper or think for one minute you are going to remember whether it was 1.5 part manure in one, or 2.5 parts sand in another. Write directly on the frame! Smooth out the mix with a trowel or a yogurt lid. Let it dry. Don't move the panels unless you have to.

Telltale signs your mix is off? Lots of cracking. Any cracking really is no good, so find one that did not crack. It is normal for the plaster to pull away from the sides of the frame, but you want a minimal amount of shrinkage; any more than $\frac{1}{16}$ to $\frac{1}{8}$ of an inch is too much. Like the test brick, rub the panels and scratch them; get a feel for the material. You'll will know the right one when you see it and feel it.

Summary

Combining the jar test and the brick test or panels is the most accurate way to find the right mix for the situation at hand. Once you know the clay content of your soil, you can estimate what the right mix is. The tests verify or help you reevaluate your theory.

Sand, Sand, and Sand

Cob and plasters are mostly made of sand ... sand held together with just the right amount of sticky stuff and the right kind of fiber to knit the masonry material in place.

Cob sand should be sharp and all different sized particles from gravel all the way down to fines. This makes sure that all empty spaces can be filled. Everything clicks together: the sharp angles lock to create a final structure that is a lot like a well-built rock wall, in miniature. The sand particles are mortared together by the clay which connects each grain to the other, holding them in place.

If you find a bank of sand and you want to harvest it, use it. Don't worry if it is all superfine and you are building tall walls. Just add some additional gravel or pea-sized sand to diversify your mix and help it click together, giving your structure the great compressive strength cob is famous for. Or, build your tall wall in stages; don't build more than two feet up at a time until the stuff below is hard, completely set.

For plasters — the thinner the layer of plaster, the finer you want the sand to be. TIP: It is well worth buying fancier fine sands by the bag when doing final coats, because sifting sand through a window screen in the rain is tedious, and the screens always seem to break.

If you a have an aggregate supply store near you, stop by and ask to have a look at the different types. Sometimes they have them on display in the grungy front office. Don't be intimidated by it all; be a newbie, be weird, don't worry about looking stupid; it is better than getting the wrong stuff delivered to your site.

Fiber

The fiber or straw in cob creates *tensile strength*. This is the ability of something to withstand sideways pull pressures, the strength something has before it is pulled apart. Tensile strength is different from *shear strength*, which represents how hard it is to cut something or make it slide against itself before it fails. Dental floss, for example, has great tensile strength — you can't pull it apart — but low shear strength — it's easy to cut.

Fiber can be so many things. We use straw in cob because it is easily available from farms or feed supply stores. We have also heard of people using canary reed grass, hemp, and dried nettle stalks. When you are building cob, you want the fibers to be as long as possible. Bales aren't what they used to be, sometimes straw can get pretty chopped up before it's baled, so check your straw... In BC we don't live in a major grain-growing region — we don't actually have a ton of options. We use what we can get.

Straw can also be used as infill (see Chapter 10, "Light Clay Walls"). The straw is tossed in clay slip and smooshed into wall cavities and plastered over. One of the properties of straw is that it is insulative. The long hollow stalks provide tons of the tiny air spaces that are the essence of any insulation, simply by trapping air to resist conductive airflow. Light clay straw has an insulation value of approximately R2 per inch, so conventional 2×6 framing does not provide sufficient insulation here in the Great White North. To achieve a more insulative wall, just frame out the walls thicker.

For plasters, there are many more options for fibers. We have used the following with varying success from best to worst:

> Manure
> Chopped straw
> Hemp hurds
> Human hair (Hyper-local! But creepy)
> Deer hair
> Dog hair and cat hair
> Feathers
> Sheeps' wool

For final finish plasters we have used:

> Paper pulp
> Cattail fluff

Lumber

Trees

When harvesting wood from the forest, we are looking for trees that are straight, don't have too many branches, and have a consistent circumference along the desired length. We have an abundance of Douglas-fir and western redcedar on our coasts. We try to use cedar for posts for two main reasons: cedar is extremely rot resistant; as posts are near the ground and sometimes run below grade, this natural feature comes in handy. Cedar also has *good compression strength*. This means it can hold a lot of straight-down pressure without buckling. We use fir for beams, joists, and rafters because it has a *high bending strength*; this means it can withstand large amounts of pressure perpendicular to the grain. Fir, while not nearly as rot-resistant, has very high compressive strength as well, so feel free to use it for posts if cedar is too expensive or hard to find.

If at all possible, cut down trees in the early spring when the running sap makes peeling the logs so much easier. If you peel a log within a few weeks of falling it, you will find the job enjoyable, not painstakingly hard and frustrating. Store your logs off the ground to keep them clean and dry — away from bacteria that live in the soil.

Many people ask if we wait for the trees to be seasoned before we build with them. We don't. We build with sections of fresh whole trees all the time. Wood in the round can check and shrink a bit, so the only exception to this practice would be cordwood walls, where the wood is used for infill, not for its structural strength. Otherwise, keeping the wood in its natural tree shape makes extremely strong and sound structures.

Dimensional Lumber

Dimensional lumber is often preferable or necessary when making up a roof skeleton or for any light clay infill framing, because of its consistency. It's really nice to get it from a local mill if you can. (From the dump or a teardown — even better.) Millers' prices can't usually compete with the lumber stores, but the quality will be higher and you also know that you are not contributing to industrial deforestation. Timber companies are only in business for grand profits; if you can avoid feeding that monster, do it. If you figure out how much you are saving using cob or light clay infill by calculating the fact you won't need additional insulation, tar paper, plastic, exterior siding, and drywall, the extra expense for local lumber will probably work itself out. You may even end up having built cheaper than your conventional neighbor.

When buying dimensional lumber, choose your boards well. Look through the piles, choose the clearest boards, the straight ones. Watch out for cracks at the ends and knots that look like they will fall out.

Mud Tools

Lumber tarps — in British Columbia, lumber is wrapped in super-strong tarp that gets discarded after the woodpile is sold. These wrappers are free, huge, and one of our best resources. Don't be afraid to ask for them at the lumber yard. Remember to pull out all the giant staples before you do any cob stomping on them!

Shovels
Pick
Mattock
Wheelbarrow
Sifting screens
Digging bar
Sledgehammer
Cob saw (aka old crappy saw)
Hammer
Crappy measuring tape
Four-foot, two-foot, and six-inch levels
Trowels (or trimmed yogurt lids)
Buckets of all sizes — but get lots around the three- to five-gallon size
Ladders and/or scaffolding

Woodworking Tools

Hammer
Saw (circular and hand)
Measuring tape
Chisel
Square
Levels (six-inch and four-foot)
Hacksaw
Ratchet set for bolt tightening
Drill
Impact driver
Bevel

Mallet
Froe (for splitting cedar)
Drawknife or spud for debarking

What Kind of Trowel to Use and Why

As you become more versed in plaster application, you will soon see how the right tools can really do a better job in experienced hands (disclaimer: for most of our plastering history, we used three plastering tools: hands for applying, a regular metal square trowel, and yogurt lids with the edges cut off for smoothing). You can do wonders with just these three things. But if you're on your way to doing this for a living or are embarking on a big project yourself, we do have some tips on which trowels are the best to use for each situation. We order good-quality Japanese trowels from LanderLand.[1] They're great for natural plasters.

Even so, we don't hesitate to use our bare hands to apply mud onto uneven surfaces like bales or funny undulating cob, and yogurt lids are still great for window recesses, alcoves, and around bottle features. Nothing else gets into the tight curves, or contours to your hand like them.

There are three workhorse trowels in our tool box :

Large Rigid Trowel (240mm)

This one is for applying an initial coat of finish material to your walls or for spreading mud over a floor surface. It's very good for getting material evenly onto a slightly undulating flat surface, as it does not flex into divots nor bend over a rise. It's not very good for curved surfaces, as it can gouge instead of follow the contour. Your local hardware store will have a standard rectangular trowel in stock. Most of us have come to prefer our Japanese ones with pointed tips — they get into smaller spaces, and gouge less.

Medium to Large Flexible Trowel (210mm)

This trowel is great for moving material around curved surfaces — those big straw bale window recesses, the nooks and crannies; it's also good for compressing and burnishing/smoothing out plasters, or if you do a lot of flat walls in a finish/fine plaster. A *large flexible trowel* gets the job done faster. If you were to use a rigid trowel for finish plaster, you could "burn" the surface — overworking can lead to cracking and discoloration. Yogurt-lid trowels are also good for compression and smoothing, but they can leave marks on the mud if the wall isn't set enough before you compress — you can avoid this if you use the flexible metal trowels instead.

The *medium flexible trowel* is better for all-around use in natural homes where there are many curves and smaller areas that need a more maneuverable tool.

Flexible Mini Trowel (120mm)

This one is an extra. She is cute, small, and flexible, perfect for going over an initial application and cleaning up trowel marks, getting into tight spaces, smoothing out transitions from one day's work to the next. She can compress a surface when necessary. This is the newest addition to most of our tool boxes, and it is much loved.

There are many other trowels out there, and many kinds of finishes. Other than those cool bent ones that are like pointed butter knives with a right angle (good for super skinny gaps around light switches and the like), they aren't absolutely necessary.

Chapter 9:

Recipes

Clay Paint Recipes That Work

THESE PAINT RECIPES NEVER LET US DOWN. They work great over basic earthen plasters, and they hold color well. The more whitening you add, the more paste you can add, too.

Paint #1

    2 parts kaolin clay
(It's bagged, sifted, and such a light color that won't darken any pigment you add to it)

    1 part starch paste
(Also known as wheat paste, paper-mache glue, wallpaper paste, or just "glue." Starch paste just sounds super professional.) See later in this chapter for recipe.

    ½ part calcium carbonate
(Also known as whitening, or that chalk stuff that they use to draw lines on soccer fields; it's like superfine powdered sand.)

Add water slowly and carefully until it reaches the consistency of paint.

Recipe

Recipe

Paint #2

> 1 part kaolin
>
> 1 part superfine sand, 325 mesh is good (available at pottery supply stores)
>
> ½ –1 part starch paste

Add water slowly and carefully until it reaches the consistency of paint.

Pigment

If pigment is in powder form, mix it with water in a jar, screw the lid on super tight, and shake it up. If you add a drop of liquid dish soap, it helps disperse the powder throughout the water. Let it sit until the pigment settles to the bottom of the jar, then gently pour off the water and measure out the pigment paste. You can also just throw the water and pigment into the mix together — just keep notes and keep everything consistent if you're trying to replicate shades over multiple mixes. You can measure pigments by volume, but if you're after maximum precision, you should weigh your pigments on a scale to really know how much you're adding each time.

Adhesion Coats

When plastering on surfaces without sufficient roughness for the plaster to mechanically grip onto the wall, like drywall or wood, here's an easy adhesive or toothy preparation coat.

> a handful of sand mixed into a bucket with
>
> 1 part conventional wood glue
>
> 2 parts water, or equal parts starch paste to water

The sand will constantly be trying to settle, so keep mixing every time you dip the paint brush. If you need a little more umph to the adhesive coat, add a handful of sifted manure. To prep a wall for lime plaster, use lime water or lime wash instead of water.

Lime Water, Lime Wash

Fill a small bucket half full of water, add enough hydrated lime powder to leave a couple of inches of water above the lime. Mix this together. The lime will begin to settle and turn into putty; some of the water will sit on top of this putty. This is what we have been calling the *lime water*. The putty mixed with more water and mixed to a paint consistency we call *lime wash*.

Starch Paste (Wheat Paste)

The starch in flour makes a good glue when heated, and has been used as a natural adhesive for thousands of years all over the world. As an additive to earthen plasters, it helps minimize particles dusting off if people or clothing brush up against walls.

Whisk together 2 cups white wheat flour and 4 cups cold water until it resembles a thin batter (like crepes or something you deep-fry — yum)

Bring 12 cups water to a rapid boil in a large pot

While boiling, add 2 tbsp borax to boiling water until dissolved. (This step is optional but helps keep the paste from going moldy as quickly. Don't keep paste for longer than a few days.)

Slowly add flour/water mix to boiling water, stirring constantly.

Take off heat and stir until the paste becomes thick and slightly translucent. (Flour burns easily!)

Let your paste cool before you mix it into your plaster.

Plasters

Plasters are the protective and beautifying skin on your walls, and they come in as many variations as walls do. We would truly love to gift you with a perfect, never-fail recipe, but we haven't found one yet. We'll

Recipe

let you know if we ever do, but every situation is different because the materials are always subtly different. Testing your plasters is the answer.

Plasters are generally made up of a binder (clay or lime), a strengthener (sand), and a fiber for tensile/shear strength.

When creating plasters (see "Test Panels" in Chapter 8), you are trying to achieve a balance between a mix that doesn't crack from excess clay, and one that doesn't "dust" from not enough clay — if the plaster doesn't have enough clay to stick all the particles together, sand will work loose from your walls when you brush up against them. Dustiness can also be reduced by other additives like starch paste. Plasters can be left to ferment, which can make them stickier ... and smellier! Every natural builder has their favorite recipes and additives, these are your starter recipes. Experiment!

Manure Plaster

We love fresh horse manure as a fiber in plasters. Manure is just concentrated fiber with the added bonus of magical beneficial enzymes.

In our area of BC, there are many horse farms and stables — lots of free poop to go around. Manure plasters are thick, sticky, and durable, making them a great base coat for the exterior and interior walls of earthen structures. It is also the perfect material for sculpting and changing your flat wall into something completely different and exciting. If you aren't a fan of the smell, don't worry, it disappears once dry. And if you don't use it all, your garden will love it. It's a great resource.

1 part clay. If using "wild clay" (dug up from the Earth), see "Clay Sourcing Tips" and "How to Test Your Clay" in Chapter 8 to figure out how

Sculptable manure plaster turns this cob oven into a dragon egg.

Recipe

much sand you will need to amend your mix properly. If using a pure source, like bagged clay or scrap potters clay, just keep it to one part of the mix, and adjust everything else around it.

2–3 parts sifted masonry sand (depending on your test results)

¾–1 part horse manure, sifted/grated through a ½-inch wire mesh screen.

Water to desired consistency — something between cake and cookie batter. For sculpting shapes, you'll want it thicker.

Clay Plaster

This is a good clay plaster recipe for interiors when you either don't have wild clay, or you want a light plaster base with added pigment. Add a bit of starch paste to cut any dusting.

2 parts sifted masonry sand (we've also used recycled crushed glass sand and bagged dolomite sand)

1 part clay (bagged EPK kaolin is cheap, and it has a nice light eggshell color)

½ part chopped fiber (finely chopped straw / shredded and soaked newspaper pulp / hemp hurds / we even used cat hair once. Allergy alert.)

¼ part starch paste

pigment

Lime Plaster

It says simple, but this isn't really simple at all. Lime has a strong personality. Lime likes to be on top of lime; it makes a bit of an electric charge and holds onto itself, and that is a beautiful relationship. Lime really loves itself! That's a lesson we can all learn. Generally lime plaster should be applied in several coats, over walls that already have a bit of lime in them.

Recipe

Unlike clay walls, which absorb and dissipate moisture, therefore grow and shrink, lime walls cannot do that, and don't really want to do that either. Lime also likes to cure, not dry. While curing, it often needs to be misted, like a beautiful orchid. Lime mustn't dry too quickly. Ideally, lime plaster should never be in full sun on a hot day while it is curing. You can hang tarps to keep the worst of the blazing heat off if necessary. It is also important to wet the heck out of the previous layer, do it the night before, the morning of, and right before you apply the fresh coat.

Lime also doesn't really like to be messed with. Don't touch it too much, or it gets a bit angry and can delaminate (peel off) or crack. Little cracks can be beautiful, but big cracks can destroy the integrity of the plaster and expose the wall underneath to unwanted moisture. Also, lime is really alkaline and can burn your skin. Wear long rubber gloves, keep acidic antidotes like vinegar or lemon close at hand to rinse exposed skin, wear glasses when mixing, and a mask so you don't breathe lime dust in. Respect the lime. Safety first.

2½ parts sand (sifted and of various tiny sizes. Dolomite sand is awesome as it is chemically similar to limestone.)

1 part lime putty (We generally use type S, a hydrated lime, as it is what is available to us here. Pour water in a large bucket and add lime to the water, mix it well and let it sit. This will become your putty.)

¼ or more part sifted fiber (straw, manure, or whatever else you want to experiment with; soaking the fiber beforehand helps to work it in the plaster)

⅛ part casein powder (to add strength and lessen dusting, you can use powdered milk, it works great and is readily available at the local grocers)

Less than 10% total volume lime-safe pigments

Chapter 10:

Tips to Success
(We Screwed Up and Learned Stuff)

Dry Stack Rock Foundation Tips

WE LIKE TO SAY that you can only move as fast or as slow as the material you are using has taken to form into its current state. Transferred from the geologic to the human scale, for example, a tree grows for some years before it's cut — building with wood can be done reasonably quickly. Rocks, on the other hand, take millennia to become rocks; therefore, we move them slowly, and build with them slowly.

When building rock foundations without mortar, we are relying on the rocks themselves for structural integrity. As a new builder, it's tempting to use mortar as a crutch for rocks that don't quite fit together well. The end result can be that a whole foundation is overly dependent on the stability of mortar. In an earthquake zone, that's no stability at all. The ground moves, the rocks move and work loose from their bond, the whole thing can fall to pieces.

Before we start, we lay out the gathered stone so we can assess all the angles and edges, making it easier to match the perfect rock to the perfect spot. You walk around with an empty space, a void of a certain shape and size in your mind. When the rocks are laid out, you can easily spot the rock that might fit your void.

We begin by placing the first course of rocks on top of a bit of sand; sand helps position rocks flat onto the ground. We begin in one spot and move along the wall, or foundation. Building with big stones, laying them side by side until they fit.

We're normally moving rocks in silence (or muttering curses under our breath). There is a zen about this process that is really special. It's all spatial relations and puzzle pieces. We try to keep the top of this first course nice and level, or at least even at the edges; jagged ups and downs are very difficult to build on top of.

Once we have a successful bottom row, we place the next course, overlapping the breaks between stones. We refer to this as a *running bond*. If the stones have edges where water might land, imagine where the water could flow, and try to influence that water to run off and away, rather than into the wall. After every course, it's best to wiggle all the rocks to make sure there is minimal movement. Make sure each rock has at least three points of contact with the rock beneath it. We use shims or "supportive friends" to stop the small wiggles, these are generally wedge-shaped or triangular smaller rocks. Keep your eyes open for those if you are finding your rocks in the wild. It is important to have a big selection to choose from, as you have no idea what voids will need filling (sounds like my date last night). Hammering the shims into place if possible is nice to insure they are secure. We build the stone wall high enough above ground height to insure the cob walls that sit atop won't get rain splashing back up on them from the ground.

Keep an eye out for shin cutters and ankle slicers; rocks can have razor edges right at leg height. Try to angle your stones so that they don't bite back. Sometimes chisels or three-pound hammers work for taking the tips off unruly stones. Be sure to wear safety glasses.

Dry stack foundation and simple post and beam skeleton, all ready for the cob.

Sometimes you will come across a beautiful rock — keep these for the perfect place by a doorframe or window, or where they might be most appreciated.

Dry Stack Rock Foundations for Straw Bale Walls

Dry stack foundations are perfect for cob walls. The final course of rocks can be left very uneven on top — it gives the cob a place to settle in and hang out. Straw bales, on the other hand, prefer a nice wide flat surface to live on. Here is how you can still have dry stack as your foundation and have a stable starting point for straw bales.

1) Once you have the rocks up to the desired height above grade (18 inches ideally), you can rent a rock drill, use a ½-inch drill bit, and drill 4–6-inches straight down into a larger rock in the center of the foundation, every 6–8 feet along the wall. (Every second bale is good).

Dry stack rock foundation with a cob bond beam for straw bales.

2) Into this hole, you can pour Rockite® or another quick-set masonry cement, and insert either rebar or threaded steel rod into each hole. The bales will be impaled on these rods. Leave these long for now, cutting them later with a hacksaw or a grinder. Follow the adhesive product's instructions for temperature ranges and set times.

3) Once the cement has set, you can proceed to build a layer of cob — no thinner than six inches — as a *bond beam*. As the rock wall undulates along the length and width, the cob thickness will also vary. Build it up until you have a level surface. Use a four-foot level on a long straight piece of 2×4 to make sure, all the way around. If you can get your hands on a laser level, you will be even more accurate.

4) Once you have your cob layer, you can start stacking bales to your heart's content ... or until your hands bleed, whichever comes first.

How to Fix Cracks

There is a crack in everything. That's how the mice get in.

— Leonard Cohen via Mudgirls

Clay is motion. With water it swells, with heat it shrinks. All this moving is wonderful as it regulates moisture, creating comfortable climates — cooling the heat of the summer and holding the warmth of the stove in the winter. Natural plasters in a bathroom or kitchen help regulate precipitation and keep mirrors from fogging up. Clay really is amazing stuff.

Earthen finishes can crack. We can think of the cracks as the beautiful details of the handmade and natural ... tiny little breathing spaces.

Sometimes, however, the beautiful little fissures are too big to be doing their job; earthen finishes are meant to create a skin that will keep droplets of moisture out, while letting water vapor pass right through.

When your cracks are too big, it is best to understand what caused them. This will depend on what you are working on.

Floors

Floors consist of a large area of moist material that will crack when not dried uniformly, or crack where there's an intentional break in the floor (thresholds between rooms). Floors require a slightly different mix than walls or plasters — making the mix a bit sandier will help prevent cracking, as will applying the layer in a uniform thickness, making use of dehumidifiers and fans to dry floors evenly, and being extra careful when filling in breaks. Compressing and hard troweling the floor when it is almost or just dry is also beneficial. (See Chapter 8 "What Kind of Trowel to Use and Why.")

Even then, some cracks are likely to appear. When fixing cracks in floors

1) Rough up the edges of the cracks

2) Dig out a v-shaped groove

3) Dampen the groove

4) Fill it in with a bit more floor mix

5) Trowel the floor smooth

When cracks are repaired and dried, a thin color wash on the floor will cover any marks made during the repair. Apply the wash before oiling and waxing the floor. When the floor cracks are super small, they can be filled with extra wax and oil. A good melted crayon can do wonders.

Clay Plaster

Clay plasters crack when the mix is a bit off, or because new buildings can settle and shift — or where there's a transition between two different surfaces. If plaster hasn't enough fiber or has too much clay, it can crack. Mixing in more sand, powdered milk, or extra sticky binders like wheat paste and cactus juice can prevent this, as will using a mesh fabric, like burlap, over transitions. Clay plasters can be wetted again using a light misting bottle or a sponge, and the plaster can generally be worked and compressed again, fixing cracks. Blend the fix by rehydrating the surrounding area and working it all together gently with a soft plastic trowel. A recycled yogurt container lid with the edges cut off is the best soft plastic trowel in our tool boxes. Be wary of over-working/compressing the area as it can leave darkened, smudgy "burn marks" on your surface that remain obvious.

Lime Plaster

Lime plasters are a slightly more serious business, as lime plaster can crack easily. If the plaster is still fresh, mist and scratch the cracks a bit, like how we open floor cracks with a slight v-shaped groove; a knife or trowel can help here. Using the same lime plaster mix, add a bit of water, and strain the plaster through cheesecloth to remove the bigger sand pieces, put the blob of new wet plaster on something that will absorb the excess water, like cardboard. This creates a lime plaster putty that can then be added to the slightly v'd-out grooves. Now, use your little plastic yogurt lid trowel to compress the area. Once dry, you can then use superfine sandpaper to smooth your fix.

If your lime plaster is already compressed and cured, the cracks can be sanded first, fixed as above, then sanded again.

Why Cob Walls Fall
Too Quick, Too Dirty, Too Thin, Too Wet

Falling walls are probably the single most dangerous thing that can happen at a cob building workshop. It's imperative that you understand the factors that can lead to it happening. If walls fall, it's because we are pushing our physical limits and the material's limit. We like to do this a bit, but failure means that we were pushing way past, really pushing the limit. The workshop is in full swing, people are getting the hang of it, there is a lot of mud going on fast, but the mix feels just a bit too sandy, it's raining like crazy, and has been for two days. There may be too many bottles going in close together, and the walls are not coming back out plumb. What we really want is to be inside drinking a coffee.

This is the most dangerous of combinations: being a bit distracted or too into it — carried away by the spirit and momentum. Any of those factors alone is not enough to topple a wall, but the combination is trouble. We have learned the hard way to check and double-check all of the forms that are being used to support window or door arches while they dry. Ask a friend to check your forms. Go around and check wall plumbness and forms at the beginning of every day, and keep checking.

If a wall falls, make sure everyone on the site is alright, take a few deep breaths, and check out the damage. That cob is still good — it might need a bit more clay, or to dry out a bit, but you can put it right back up on the wall when you're ready.

> Mudgirl Amanda-Rae put together a wall fall playlist for you. These might not be appropriate to play if your clients are right there …
>
> Bastille — "Pompeii"
>
> Bedouin Soundclash — "Walls Fall Down"
>
> Anias Mitchell — "Coming Down"
>
> Tom Petty and the Heartbreakers — "Walls"
>
> John Cougar Mellencamp — "Crumblin' Down"
>
> Rancid — "Fall Back Down"
>
> Beck — "Walls"
>
> Travelling Wilburys — "Tweeter and the Monkey Man"
>
> Ani DiFranco — "Buildings and Bridges"

Recapping Reasons Why Walls Fall

- Mix is too wet, the weather is too wet, the wall beneath can't hold the weight of the fresh cob and it slips out, the rest of the wall goes with it.
- Wall heading out of plumb. The wall ends up not centered over the foundation.
- Wall getting wider as it goes up, becoming top-heavy.
- Arch supports are not built correctly, and the weight of the wet cob collapses it.
- Cob lacks quality clay to properly glue the mix together.
- Too much decoration in the wall. Too many bottles or alcoves in a wall that's too thin can lead to instability.
- Wall going up too fast. Don't lay on a new course of cob if the layer below is sploogy jelly. Let it set up. Four feet per day is usually the very most you should expect to put on any one spot.

- The number one factor: lack of care and attention to the cob walls as they are being built.

Wall Systems Pros and Cons

Whatever the walls are made of:

- The building will need a roof as soon as possible to protect the natural materials until the finishing is complete. As the old cobbers say: "Give it a good hat and boots." The roof is your hat. Think large overhangs. Think wraparound porch!
- Natural buildings require a high foundation — at least 18 inches above grade — to keep water from wicking up into the walls and to prevent drip line splash back. (This would be your boots.)
- All finishing renders or plasters must be made of a breathable material; this keeps the moisture that's always in the air moving freely in and out of the wall system. It also allows water to be dispersed and dried out quickly when the walls do get some sideways rain.

   Note: Cement is not breathable and is NOT an appropriate plaster over natural materials.

A building made of natural materials will not melt if it gets wet. This is a common misconception. If it gets wet, natural plaster spreads out the moisture — the wall will dry out with the breeze. Mind you, if a wind-blown drip off your roof beats against a building repeatedly in one spot, it will eventually gouge a groove into the protective plaster. Even so, you'll notice this damage well before erosion affects the actual wall, and it is easily fixed. Put up gutters and carry that precious water where it's needed.

When deciding which wall system to go with, consider the roof. Cob and straw bale walls are conducive to load-bearing structures (which means the actual walls are supporting the roof, instead of posts and beams). Building with load-bearing walls also means you don't have a roof until the walls are all the way up. For this reason, we advise people to consider a post and beam structure for all wall systems, to insure that a roof is on before the first winter. A roof is also pretty nice to work and to store materials under, if you have a rainy building season. A temporary roof with tarps and light wood is not secure in high winds or torrential rain — if the wind doesn't tear it apart, tarps are guaranteed to eventually gather water. Especially if you aren't living on your building site to babysit the walls and the materials, a roof can be a wonderful thing.

Light Clay Walls

Light Clay Pros

Light clay infill is one of the most adaptable forms of natural building we have come across. It lends itself well to conventional building; in fact we consider it to be the bridge between two worlds. Light clay walls are built much like conventional stud walls; the foundations are similar, the roof, the whole thing can end up looking a lot like a regular house. Now, to this we'd normally say "whoop-dee-freakin-do, we aren't in this to make things that look normal".... But the idea that all natural buildings don't have to look like you stepped out of The Shire can be refreshing for some.

The other plus is that light clay walls do not have to have a continuous foundation. If proper support is in place, this wall system can be off the ground altogether on a post and pad foundation, and this design can save a lot of time, which can translate into money. These wall systems can use a variety of materials for the infill. Straw is common, as are wood chips, hemp, or any combination of these. The clay you need does not have to be pure, but 70% or higher, turned into a paint-like "slip," is good. The mixing is light work and easy to insert into the wall cavity; it does not require pneumatic tampers or any loud machinery. This wall system negates the need for additional insulation, drywall, vapor barrier, exterior cladding, tar paper, plywood ... you can see how much money this would save, and how much it would lower the carbon footprint of your build.

Light Clay Cons

This system of wall does require a general understanding of conventional framing, so carpentry skills and tools are well put to use here.

You need to know how to frame out windows and doors, and depending on your roof design, build a *rake wall* (the top plate of your wall slopes upwards to create the roof shape). Also, it's best to use dimensional lumber to frame everything; this can increase price, and could impose do-it-yourself-off-your-land limitations.

The system requires a long drying time, about a week per inch of infill. So depending on your climate, this could be a limiting factor or not. Here on the wet coast, we want to be filling those ten-inch walls before August 1st — even earlier if possible. The outer walls need at least one good coat of plaster before the weather shifts into the rainy season. These walls are sensitive to weather if left exposed.

Cob Walls

Cob Wall Pros

Cob is wonderful, sculptable, fairly foolproof, and super easy to learn. This material is cheap and abundant; you don't need special skills to sculpt something out of clay, sand, and straw. You can use recycled windows easily — they can be placed right into the cob and don't need a frame unless they are going to be openers. Every cob house is unique and built to suit the folks who will live there. The many opportunities for personal touches are a big part of the draw.

Cob buildings have an extremely feminine feeling. The curves, the deep darkness of the earth, the decorative aspects are a reflection of this. A cob building is thermal mass, which can be a pro or a con depending on its use, location, and placement. Building with cob can seem daunting if your priority is just to get 'er done, but tapping into your community or a Mudgirls workshop changes the building process into something much more amazing. There's no need for heavy machinery. Hand tools, buckets, shovels, and tarps are just about all you need to get started. For folks who are just setting out on the journey of natural building, cob is often the best place to begin.

The structure that holds up your roof can be made out of unmilled raw logs in the round, and can be very simple because cob is monolithic and creates bracing for the entire building if the posts are partly or wholly enveloped in the walls.

When your walls are done, your walls are done. They'll want at least one layer of plaster to protect and beautify, but unlike light clay and straw bale walls, they can handle some weather without damage or rotting.

Cob Wall Cons

With its handbuilt, gang-built nature (often by those new to the craft), and the very way in which you build the walls (from the bottom up), we have found that you can't be too attached to precision. Having perfectly matching alcoves on either side of a window can be difficult to achieve: symmetry can be challenging.

The lack or inability to maintain complete control, the letting go of a definite outcome, leads to a sense of wonder and trust in the process that can be wildly liberating. In our experience, the people who manage to keep the big picture in their minds instead of being focused on the minutiae have a much more enjoyable time and find that, in the end, everything is as it should be. There is a freedom in this that envelops people as they realize that the plan has altered. At first they

Taking time for precision amid the chaos.
CREDIT: BRIANNA WALKER

Space-saving ladder to loft.

get dishevelled, then realize there is a whole world of influences that are beyond our control. You see them visibly relax and go one step at a time.

Cob is not insulative, so a largish house exclusively made out of cob will be hard to heat. Design your house accordingly.

Cob walls are heavy, and they must be completely supported by a foundation. This requires more material and can add to costs/time. But if you have time, you don't need money ....

Straw Bale Walls

Straw Bale Pros

Straw bale buildings have super insulative value. Everywhere in Canada but southwestern BC, this is the best choice for all your walls — or at least the north and east walls. (Light clay systems are good too, but you would have to have figure out what your local insulation requirements are to decide the width.) Straw bale walls go up quickly once the foundation and any supporting structure is complete. The wooden roof support structure can also be simple and created out of raw logs. Straw (a waste product from the grain industry) is abundant in many parts of North America.

A common misconception is that straw houses are more combustible than conventional housing. This is just not the case. There is very little oxygen in these walls, and fire needs air. Try lighting an urban phone book on fire: you can singe the edges, but without gasoline or a blowtorch you would be hard pressed to really ignite it. Just keep the gasoline off your straw bale walls, don't let your kids use the blowtorch, and you should fare well.

Straw Bale Cons

When your walls are done, they are not done. Straw bales require the most amount of finishing work. You need to stuff cavities between the bales, and it's best to cover both inside and outside surfaces with clay slip before you even begin plastering. Then you need at least two coats of plaster (most need three or more if you want flat walls). The areas around windows will likely need shaving or stuffing to create the desired bevelled, deep-set window boxes that are so indicative of straw bale homes.

It is best to have a continuous foundation for these wall systems, but we have seen it done successfully on a post and pad. You need to insure you have very sturdy and wide supports for your walls in this case.

Build Your House in Ten Steps!

This is a big picture overview, to help demystify the building process. There is lots to know about building a house. It can seem daunting even if you are not going to be the lead builder, designer, materials gatherer, hole digger. If you are taking on building your own small home for you and for your family, the challenges may seem insurmountable. The Mudgirls are here to assure you that it is not. You can do it, you just need to know a few things first:

1) Build small — it will save your budget and your marriage (if you have one)
2) Build for warmth
3) Most importantly — ask for help

Natural materials are very forgiving, and making mistakes is part of the building process. Nothing will teach you more than the mistakes that are guaranteed to occur, but don't let that stop you. Plus it's fun to figure stuff out!

We often build simple post and beam frames, with dry stack foundations, and a natural wall system. The instructions that follow are based on the Mudgirl-patented "cob rocket,"[1] but can incorporate other wall systems, as nature dictates!

Step 1: Draw Some Pictures

Get some of those ideas on paper. General floor plan and elevations from the front, back, and sides. How many rooms, levels, exits? What does the roofline look like? Can you build just the essentials — a kitchen and bedrooms, and expand at a later date when money and time are more in your favor?

What will the walls be made of? Cob, light clay, straw bale, cordwood, earthbag? Why? Are you making the choice because it is the coolest newest thing or because it is the right material for your climate and resource availability? What will you roof be made of? Living roof, metal, tires; these can require different pitches. Living roofs are really heavy and require a more girthy structure underneath.

Step 2: Find a Location

Where does the sun rise in the winter, in the summer? Where do the prevailing winds come from? Are there trees? Do they protect us, shade us? What is the site like at its hottest, coldest, wettest?

Work with nature, don't make more work by struggling needlessly against it. Don't build it in the best food-growing location. Grow food there instead.

Step 3: Clear the Site

Clear it bigger than your actual house footprint, leaving room for perimeter drains. Dig down at least to the subsoil, and as deep as the local frostline dictates. Put the topsoil you have removed on your garden plot.

How is the water from the roof, or from other parts of the land, going to move away from your house? Think about the gutters and perimeter drains. What are you building your foundation out of? It needs to be 18 inches above grade when completed. Do you need gravel to backfill your site for drainage and to make it level before you lay your first course of foundation rocks? See "Dry Stack Rock Foundation Tips," earlier in this chapter.

Mark out your exterior wall on the ground. Mark where your posts will go. Square it all up. Lay post rocks first — find nice big flat ones six inches or more thick; lay them in a bed of sand so that they nestle nicely and are stable once placed. You can drill into the rock to set rebar or a metal bracket using a quick-setting rock adhesive: insert this anchor into the rock right in the middle of where the post will sit. Having six inches of rebar protruding above the rock is good.

Step 4: The Structure

You know where your posts are going. Do you know how high they need to be? Remember to account for the fact that the bottom of your post is below final floor level — don't forget to add that difference to your post height. Where are the loft beams in relation to the final floor height? Where are the roof beams in relation to the loft floor? Remember to leave yourself enough head room!

Figure out how you are going to connect the posts and beams together. Ask someone you know who isn't going to disempower you, or you can read up on it. Keep it simple, keep it strong. Impale your post on its metal thing. Brace it three ways, like a triangle. Pound stakes into the ground going in the opposite direction of the braces, screw that shit together using two screws. At this stage you can attach your loft beams, then

Sexy trenches. It might be draining, but it's important (groan).

floor joists, then upper floor sheathing. From there, you can frame the upstairs, or the posts could continue up to the roof. Place the roof beams and run the rafters across them. If you are new to house building, build a single story for safety and for sanity. Between the first story posts, you can frame out for your infill if you have chosen a system that requires this. (Light clay walls, for example.) Because you have hefty

Post and beam structure for Rolling Earth (all beach-salvaged timber).

posts supporting your roof, your framing is not carrying any load. This is good, because you may just be learning, and your rookie framing will do just fine.

Step 5: Put Your Roof On

We cannot stress this enough. Big overhangs. No less than 24 inches on a single story, more if you want a covered front entrance, or a wall more than ten feet high. People get excited about their walls, but you have to have your roof on before the first rains return. That is mid-September where we live. At least get the skeletal structure up, before getting too far ahead of yourself with the vulnerable natural walls.

Safety First: How will you get up and down? Make sure your ladders are good, and that the scaffolding is stable. Rent them if you have to. Tool belts come in handy up there. Your best asset is a friend: someone who can hand you stuff and find good songs on the radio. Don't drop any tools on their head — get them a hard hat. Borrow a roof harness if your pitch is steep. Even if the roof isn't steep, it wouldn't hurt to be protected.

Step 6: Walls

Cob is very strong, but only once it's dry. (Read "Why Cob Walls Fall," earlier in this chapter.) Organize yourself. Have your clay, your gritty sand. Get 10–20% extra quantity. Do some math: width x length x height. You can subtract your windows and doors. Example: if your wall

Light clay farm-building workshop.

is ten feet long, one foot wide, and seven feet high you will need to make 70 cubic feet of cob. Now, if your cob is made out of 75% sand and 15% clay soil, then you will need to multiply 70 by .75 (sand) and 70 by .15 (clay) to get your raw material amounts (27 cubic feet equals 1 cubic yard). Earthen materials are often sold in yard volumes.

If you are planning on having any counters against the walls, figure out at what height you want them. Put in wall anchors — they are called *dead men*. If you are tall or short you can design according to your own body! Place empty two- to four-inch PVC pipe through your wall where your water will come in and out, where your electricity and propane will come in. What about a chimney pipe — is it going through the wall or the roof?

Call everyone you know, make posters, plan a set of dates: ten days in early summer and five to ten days more a month later. Ask a friend to do the cooking, at least the lunches. Have lots of buckets, tarps, shovels, wheelbarrows. Have all the windows on hand, make frames for them that are ½-inch too big in all directions so that you can easily place the windows within the holes later on. The ones that go right in the wall, just put them in the wall as you go — nice and level and plumb — check using a four-foot level on each window angle. Collect stout lintels to go above windows and doors, to take the weight of the cob walls that are yet to be built above. The wider the opening to be bridged, the stouter the lintel. Lintels should be the entire width of the wall. (Tip : Remember that dimensional lumber is stronger when used up on its edges rather on its wide flat sides.) Try to have lots of scrap wood on hand. Have fun, play music, have a check-in with everyone at the beginning of the workday. Have goals set out. But don't worry if you don't reach them.

Step 7: Plaster

Plaster protects and beautifies. It goes on when the walls are dry inside and out. Outside gets the weather, so focus on that first. See Chapter 9 for plaster recipes.

Inlaid hydronic pipes under a massive earthen floor.

Step 8: Close Her In

Put in framed windows and doors. Insulate the roof, and lay the floor.

Step 9: Other House Systems

Figure out a simple greywater system for your kitchen water, get some help wiring if you are scared. But there are great books out there for the easy stuff.

Step 10: Move In!

You did it. Welcome to your beautiful little handbuilt home. Now, start planning your next adventure! Cob sauna...Norwegian-style epic woodpile...world's most beautiful outhouse...cob pizza oven.... We can't wait to hear what you dream up.

Molly's house.

Endnotes

Part I

Chapter 1

1. Of course too much power has been placed in the hands of the people who control the flow of money. The issue they have with people building outside of conventional rules is *potential* lost income on the property's resale value. This argument assumes that all future buyers will share today's cookie-cutter taste in how to live. We believe that banks don't need to make so much cash, and that not everything has to get more expensive as time passes. Convincing disguises of progress and insurance regulations offer a fictional sense of safety and what seems like the worst kind of helicopter parenting — those demanding that rules be followed don't even love you or tuck you in at night. Their insistence is invasive. It may be dressed in care and protection, but it's a ruse to make sure everything flows through the capitalistic financial system so chunks of profit can be taken off at every pass. Remember what profit means: profit is not the same as income. It's the amount of money left over *after* you have paid out all your expenses, yourself, the rent, the bills; it's the money that goes into someone's pocket. In the dominant game, that pocket will not be yours.
2. Eco-sense website. [online]. [cited November 30, 2017]. eco-sense.ca.
3. This house had a huge fir tree fall on it a few years ago. The tree only crushed the top-story sleeping loft. (A conventional house would

have been completely flattened — so stated the tree falling expert who came to survey the damage.) The cob remained undamaged below. The owners were resourceful: they took the wood from the injuring tree, had it milled, and proceeded to rebuild the top story with it.

Chapter 2

1. A phrase coined by novelist Amitav Ghosh to describe humanity's insane inaction in the face of climate change: Amitav Ghosh. *The Great Derangement: Climate Change and the Unthinkable.* University of Chicago, 2016.
2. The Canelo Project website. [online]. [cited November 30, 2017]. caneloproject.com.
3. Earthen Endeavors Natural Building website. [online]. [cited November 30, 2017]. earthenendeavors.com.
4. Becky Bee. *The Cob Builder's Handbook: You Can Hand-Sculpt Your Own Home,* 3rd ed. Groundworks, 1998.
5. J.K. Gibson-Graham. *A Postcapitalist Politics.* University of Minnesota, 2006, p. 7.

Chapter 3

1. Freeda is Program Director of the Cloud Forest Institute in Ukiah, California. Their website [online]. [cited December 1, 2017]. cloudforest.org.
2. Just to be clear: it isn't that these buildings take so much longer to build — just like the slow food doesn't take longer to grow. On the contrary, our building projects are often right on schedule — winter's fast approach keeps us on target. It's merely a change in pace, a switch of focus, the decommodification of the building supply chain, avoiding the mass production lines. It's the labor of many hands guided by experience. With eyes wide open to the impact and effort at each step, it's in the preparation of the ingredients, the thoughtful bringing together of all components. Something built that way becomes not just a space to live, not just a house, but a true home that, despite its new house smell, is filled to the brim already

with memories tucked in all the nooks and crannies, deep under the foundation.

3. It's alarming to see the notion of tiny homes being transformed into boutique consumer items. If small is "cool," we're easily convinced it's okay to pay the same rent to live in a van as we used to pay to live in a one-bedroom apartment. It makes the sane idea that "smaller is better" feel like more insane bullshit. Nevertheless, the interest in tiny homes is a reflection of people's sincere desire to step outside societal forces that act on us in ways that are hard to fully comprehend; to feel a little (tiny) agency in our lives.

4. Laura Matthias. *ExtraVeganZa: Original Recipes from Phoenix Organic Farm*. New Society, 2006.

Chapter 4

1. Government of Canada. *Employment Insurance Maternity and Parental Benefits*. [online]. [cited November 14, 2017]. canada.ca/en/employment-social-development/programs/ei/ei-list/reports/maternity-parental.html#h2.1.

2. To learn more about kids and how much they need someone to love them right, read: Gordon Neufeld and Gabor Maté. *Hold On to Your Kids: Why Parents Need to Matter More Than Peers*. Ballantine, 2006.

Chapter 6

1. Compassionate Communication is work derived from Marshall Rosenberg's Nonviolent Communication. See the Compassionate Communications website [online]. [cited December 4, 2017]. compassionatecommunications.us.

Part II

Chapter 8

1. LanderLand website. [online]. [cited November 26, 2017]. japanesetrowels.com.

Chapter 10

1. We developed the cob rocket as a way of skirting building codes. In essence, if you build a structure with a small enough footprint

to be deemed "an outbuilding," you can use any materials you like. To mitigate the smallness, we build the walls up nice and high to accommodate a roomy loft. Another strategy is to bump out the second floor or loft to be wider than the ground level. Building codes only measure the footprint on the ground.

Index

adhesion coats, 144
adobe, 48
air circulation, 22–23
airtight dwellings, 22–23
alternative economies, 38, 52–53, 119–122
applied activism, 3, 4–5, 105–106

Baird, Ann and Gord, 21
bartering, 2, 89
Bee, Becky, 49
bending strength, 138
Bethany's Rice Pudding, 74
bodies, as resources, 43–45, 64
Boots-On meetings, 57, 107
breathability, 22–23
brick test, 134
British Columbia, south coastal region, 10–11, 158.
   See also Lasqueti Island.
building codes. *See* regulations, and building.

building materials, and toxicity, 20, 68
building process, ten steps, 161–167
Burnstad, Freeda Alida, 61–62

camaraderie, 37, 40, 42, 61, 105
Canelo Project, 46
capitalism, 2, 3, 24, 52, 92–93
carbon footprints, 20, 31, 157
cedar, 50, 53, 69, 70, 137–138
check-ins, 63–64, 109
childcare, 2, 13, 34–35, 38, 41, 77–88
clay, sourcing and testing, 131–135
clay paint recipes, 143–148
clay plaster, 147, 153–154
clay slip, 137, 157, 161
clients, issues with, 17–18, 35, 78–79, 89–91, 98–100, 112
climate change, 1, 14, 93–94
Cob Builder's Handbook, 49

173

About the Author

*T*HE MUDGIRLS is an all-women natural building collective from coastal British Columbia that formed in 2007. Founded on the principle of self-empowerment, they champion the use of natural, local, and salvaged materials; human-scaled DIY solutions; non-hierarchical decision-making; support for mothers; care for children; and fun. They build things and offer workshops that empower people to take back the right to provide themselves with shelter in ways that promote harmony with the Earth. The Mudgirls have collaborated with people from all over the world, forging alliances and honing the skills not only to build homes, but to build communities. Find out more at mudgirls.ca.

A Note about the Publisher

New Society Publishers is an activist, solutions-oriented publisher focused on publishing books for a world of change. Our books offer tips, tools, and insights from leading experts in sustainable building, homesteading, climate change, environment, conscientious commerce, renewable energy, and more — positive solutions for troubled times.

We're proud to hold to the highest environmental and social standards of any publisher in North America. This is why some of our books might cost a little more. We think it's worth it!

- We print all our books in North America, never overseas
- All our books are printed on **100% post-consumer recycled paper,** processed chlorine free, with low-VOC vegetable-based inks (since 2002)
- Our corporate structure is an innovative employee shareholder agreement, so we're one-third employee-owned (since 2015)
- We're carbon-neutral (since 2006)
- We're certified as a B Corporation (since 2016)

At New Society Publishers, we care deeply about *what* we publish — but also about *how* we do business.

Download our catalogue at https://newsociety.com/Our-Catalog or for a printed copy please email info@newsocietypub.com or call 1-800-567-6772 ext 111

New Society Publishers
ENVIRONMENTAL BENEFITS STATEMENT

For every 5,000 books printed, New Society saves the following resources:[1]

25	Trees
2,291	Pounds of Solid Waste
2,521	Gallons of Water
3,288	Kilowatt Hours of Electricity
4,164	Pounds of Greenhouse Gases
18	Pounds of HAPs, VOCs, and AOX Combined
6	Cubic Yards of Landfill Space

[1]Environmental benefits are calculated based on research done by the Environmental Defense Fund and other members of the Paper Task Force who study the environmental impacts of the paper industry.